Famous Wisconsin Ghosts and Ghost Hunters

Hannah Heidi Levy and Brian G. Borton

Foreword by Dennis Boyer

Badger Books Inc.
Oregon, Wis.

ISBN+10 1-932542-28-0
ISBN+13   978-1-932542-28-8

Badger Books Inc./Waubesa Press
P.O. Box 192
Oregon, WI 53575
Toll-free phone: (800) 928-2372
Fax: (608) 835-3638
Email: books@badgerbooks.com
Web site: www.badgerbooks.com

This book is dedicated to paranormal investigators, ghost hunters, and the souls who like to hang around just for the heck of it. **–Hannah Heidi Levy**

This is for my mom, Nancy Borton. **–Brian G. Borton**

Dark and Stormy
Table of Contents

Foreword by Dennis Boyer -------------------------------9
Introduction ---11

Investigative case files

1. Wausau Paranormal Research Society ---------------15
   Grand Theater, Wausau
   Another Baffling Case
   Mysterious Knocking in the Wall
   An Interview with Todd Roll and Shawn Blaschka

2. What the Unexplained Experts Tell Us --------------24
   Chad Lewis and Terry Fisk
   More Questions for the Investigator

3. Files of the Southern Wisconsin Paranormal
   Research Group -------------------------------------32
   An Interview with Jen Lauer and Dave Schumacher

4. *Weird Wisconsin* Quips and Comments -------------40
   An Interview with Linda Godfrey

5. The Ghost Lady--------------------------------------50
   An Interview with Heidi Linden

6. New Group take a S.P.I.N.--------------------------57

An interview with Amy Tomlin

7. From the Mysterious Journal
   of a Private Investigator --------------------------------61
   First, the Private Dectectvie sspeaks
   The case of the motorcycle and the anxious spirit
   The case of the ghostly lawyer
   The case of the distressed woman and the fussy Tylenol bottle
   The case of the boy and the river
   The case of the perturbed mother ghost
   A few more thoughts about the paranormal
   It's not the people buried there who are huanting the cemetery

8. Words from Kathleen Schneider, Medium
   and Psychic ---73
   Enter Kathleen
   Scott's comments
   In a recent interview with us, Kathleen said
   For the record

9. Personal Accounts Gathered by Roving
   Writer Brian Borton ----------------------------------78
   Brian Goes to the Bar Next Door
   Haunted Mickey's Tavern
   Jingles Coliseum Bar
   Ominous Ontario Street
   A Trip to Bootleggers Super Club.
   A Terrorized Cat
   Another Guest at the Party
   A Dog Named Hello?

10. Roving Writer Brian Borton asks:
    "Do you believe in ghosts?"-------------------------108
    Your Answers — Brian's Public Opinion Poll
    Cinnamon Toast
    Highway O
    Tired Ghost
    Charlie

Reflections

11. Animal Encounters with the Paranormal
    and Paranormal Animals R Us --------------------113
    What's Wisconsin without a Few Ghostly Cows?
    Wren in Bad Weather
    The Horse's Disapproval
    Big Pig Exorcism
    Pogo the Watchdog Detects Captain Gust
    Peanut the Raccoon Still Eating Sandwiches
    Transparent Chickens

12. Fact and Fiction and Legends to Ponder ---------129
    The Telling of a Tale
    Ridgeway Ghost Tales
    Le Griffon a haunted ship (Green Bay)
    Ravensholme Farm (Waukesha County)
    Summerwind (West Bay Lake, northern Wisconsin)
    T.B. Scott Mansion (Merrill)
    Marie's House (National Avenue, Milwaukee)
    Marquette University
    Whispering Oaks Restaurant
    Nashotah House
    Hasslinger's Moose Lake Beach
    Giddings Haunted Boarding House
    The steamer Chicora: Beauty of the Great Lakes
    Mary Bluth Farm
    Bedroom Curtain Ghost
    Restless Spirit
    Ramada Plaza, Fond du Lac

13. The Short Stories in a Long List ------------------194
    Touring with the Cliff Notes
    Here's another boat load of ghosts

14. End of the Story or is it? --------------------------224
        Tips on Ghost Hunting
    My house is haunted...what should I do?
        Message in a Bottle

Acknowlegments --239
Bibliography and Resources ---------------------------240

Foreword

Writing about ghosts has provided generations of writers with subject matter that is at once durable and adaptable. Our literary ghosts inhabit the classics and pulp fiction. The genre ranges from simple folktales to complexly layered letters noir exploring our dark sides.

Still, there is often a one-dimensional attitude toward ghosts in the various works of fiction, folklore, and paranormal documentation. Few of these works explore the range of questions that the possibility of inhabitants of a spirit world can rouse in the casual observer and supernatural investigator alike. Hannah Heidi Levy and Brian Borton raise these tantalizing questions and point us in some interesting directions.

Like the private investigator, which the two write about, they delve into some of society's attitudes and hidden agendas when it comes to the A, B, C's of X, Y, and Z-files. They wrestle with science, the paranormal community, history, and human psychology. But you won't find solutions all wrapped up in neat packages with a tight bow of conclusions. No, they acknowledge the unknowable and invite us to devise our own ways of finding meaning among the many ways of approaching this subject matter.

It is entirely appropriate that they focus this mix of investigation, personal accounts, ghost-hunting technique and local lore on our fair Wisconsin. The Badger State is said to boast more ghost stories per square mile than any other similarly sized expanse of cities, farms, forests, and shoreline in North America. Some say that the reports, encounters, legends, and yarns number in the tens of thousands. My own experience suggests that there is practically a story for every abandoned rural schoolhouse and neglected cheese factory, that constituting a goodly start on the thousands.

Ghosts help define a place. Ghostly accounts, whether phenomenological records or family heirloom stories, tell us much about what is important to the people who dwell in a place and, perhaps, tell us something about the people who record the accounts. Levy and Borton have made a worthy contribution to our understanding of Wisconsin's haunted cultural geography and have created an interesting new format for looking at the ghosts of a place and those who hunt them.

--Dennis Boyer

A few recent books by Dennis Boyer:
Driftless Spirits (1997)
Gone Missing (2002)
Northern Frights (1998) (2005)
Once Upon a Hex (2004)
Snow on the Rails (2003)

Introduction

The subject of ghosts is both a common and an uncommon topic. As a culture, we pursue ghosts for their ability to conjure up a chilling tale. It's macabre entertainment. It's the sensation of momentary fear with an escape hatch. It's a component of folklore-ish heritage. It beckons to explore mystery. In those ways, the subject of ghosts is universal. Less common, are the serious paranormal endeavors. Some of us study the phenomenon in an electromagnetic effort to make sense of the world, to test the waters of perhaps another dimension in the realm of physics not yet explained. But why? We don't think there's one solid answer to the question. The question might as well have something to do with why we climb the mountain. Standard answer is because it's there. Well, in the case of a ghost, most of us don't know if it's there or not.

Famous Wisconsin Ghosts and Ghost Hunters brings you a ghost book with some detours along the way. We decided to include several investigative Cases, and personal accounts from a number of sources. Roving Writer, Brian, asks, "Do you believe in ghosts?" We included a section for those who might be "barking up your own tree" titled "Animal Encounters with the Paranormal." Of course, what would a ghost book be without the Legends that abound and change slightly from year to year or generation to generation? Although, we couldn't cover every story "unearthed," we have an extensive list of possibilities.

To finish off the book, we have included the "End of Story…or is it?" This section is a brand of behind-the-scenes production. We've included "Tips on Ghost Hunting." If your house is haunted, read the "What to Do Section." Finally, there's the "Message in a Bottle."

It's important to point out that expert objective paranormal investigators really are *not* a dime a dozen. There are many hobbyists who dabble in paranormal investigation, but few who actually master the craft. The truly impartial researcher cannot emphatically declare beyond a shred of doubt that a so-called ghost is the spirit of a departed person, some sort of an imprint in time, or a naturally occurring energy manifestation. Nobody knows. Those who seriously research will be the first ones to admit this. The diligent investigators can give us their best guess impressions, but that's about it. When we sit back and think about it all, that the fact nobody knows, or may ever know, is intriguing. It's literally awesome. It's our ticket to the show, our ticket to timeless mystery, and our ticket to captivating literature and tales not yet told.

Wisconsin certainly has its ghosts. *Famous Wisconsin Ghosts and Ghost Hunters* does not do a census count, and I doubt that ghosts are required to register with any government entity or bother with other paperwork, so like a ghost; the book just is what it is. We hope you enjoy the jaunt through these pages of uncertainty. Next time you're peering out into a misty night, you might ask yourself, is it just the fog? If that's too scary, then convince yourself that it really *is* the fog. Sure, yes, exactly…that's what it is…the fog.

— **Hannah Heidi Levy**
and Brian G. Borton
Fall, 2005

Famous Wisconsin Ghosts and Ghost Hunters

Investigative Case Files

Wausau Paranormal Research Society

It was a dark and scary night, or sometimes it's a dark and stormy night. You've probably been living on Mars if you haven't heard that classic ghostly introduction to a chilling tale. Investigators of paranormal phenomenon, known to many as "ghost hunters," have checked out dozens of dark-and-scary-night places. We contacted the illustrious researchers and asked them about cases that they have investigated. Going a step further, we wanted to know about specific cases that actually fall into the category of "unexplained" phenomenon. Permit us to explain so at least not all is unexplainable. Two kinds of investigative cases exist. The majority of cases have a familiar explanation such as faulty plumbing or an outmoded electrical situation. But a few of the cases are just plain unexplainable by the most talented and objective of investigators. One such case comes to us from the Wausau Paranormal Research Society lead investigators, Shawn Blaschka and Todd Roll.

Grand Theater
Wausau, Wisconsin

The Grand Theater was built in 1927 and was home to stage plays until the 1930s-1940's when it converted to a movie theater until the late 1980's or early 1990's. Today the theater is an active home to the performing arts. It seats 1200 people, and has been restored to its old glory. However, some people suspect the venue has a resident ghost. In the 1950's came reports of film canisters moving from one place to another. The theater staff would find the canisters in odd places outside of the usual storage area. During the last twenty years, there have been reports of apparitions. Those who have seen the ghost think that it is the former theater manager, Larry Belts. He was the theater manager from around 1945 to the late 1980's, having started out as an usher in the 1930's. Larry did not die in the theater. However, he had a great love for the building and the theater life that constituted the mortar of every brick. He had a bedroom in the building, and often slept there.

Larry's alleged ghost has been spotted by actors and workers in the theater. Most have seen him as he looked at an older age, while others have seen him as a younger man in clothing characteristic of an earlier era. The apparition is reported to have been watching play practice, standing in the balcony, walking along the lighting rack above the stage, or moving through walls where doors were once located.

Wausau Paranormal Research investigated the theater on four occasions and recorded especially unusual phenomenon each time. The first investigation produced a photo of the balcony with an amorphous mass wrapped around the balcony railing. This mass was not visible to the photographer when he took the photo. On the second trip, the investigators picked up a voice on an EVP (electronic voice phenomenon) taping in the northern most spotlight room. In all clarity the voice said, "Don't go back over here." The two investigators were the only ones in the room, but a third voice ended up on the tape. Another voice, which sounded like someone whispering "21", was recorded as coming from the lighting rig above the balcony. The investigators did not know the significance of "21." Inexplicable voices on tape sound similar to a person whispering close to a microphone.

The group's third investigation concentrated on the spotlight room. A Sony camcorder with Nightshot and EMF (electromagnetic field meter) were rigged up together. The camera was monitored from a remote location one floor down from the spotlight room. Larry the ghost, or some form of energy became active at 8:20 PM.

The meter spiked, signaling the presence of an electromagnetic field, while simultaneously, a ball of light was recorded moving erratically across the screen. A temperature change was also recorded at that time.

Not finished yet, the Wausau Paranormal Research group joined with Wisconsin Ghost Investigators to enlist the opinion of a psychic who was visiting from the Milwaukee area. A psychic is not used often by these researchers. The psychic noted seeing a man on the stage, describing him in great detail. Her description was almost an exact match to Larry Belts; now possibly, ghost Larry Belts.

Another baffling case...

The Wausau Paranormal Research Society investigated an abandoned rectory in central Wisconsin on reports of paranormal activity and rumors of haunting. Cold spots, moving shadows, and tops that spun by themselves—what could be more tempting to the investigators? The group secured permission to enter the property and conducted an investigation in two rooms over the course of three visits. The power lines and water had been cut off several years earlier, which meant there were no manufactured electromagnetic fields that might interfere with readings. Despite this, electromagnetic field readings were detected, and in some cases, the field appeared to move across the room. The case remains open to the researchers, but thus far, they have found no explanation for the anomalous EMF (electromagnetic field) readings.

Mysterious knocking on the wall

If you had an upstairs bedroom, and a baffling rapping came a tapping, what would you do? Maybe write poetry. You've looked for rational answers, you've searched your mind to no end, but still the cause of the odd noise eludes you. It's getting to be annoying, and now that wave of fear creeps up on you, especially in the dark of night. Some days the noise is more persistent and louder than on other days. Perhaps hesitant to blame a culprit entity, but more frightened than anything else, you might call the ghost hunter, or in this case, the Wausau Paranormal Research Society.

True story: The owners of the house were absolutely convinced that "something" was in the house. The longer this went on, the more they attributed the rapping phenomenon to a frightening haunting. This notion exponentially escalated the family's fright. What was it? Hint: the wind blowing had something to do with the rapping. Give up? After a bit of searching and testing, the investigators came up with your basic fearsome cable TV cord hitting the side of the house when the wind blew. Simple enough, but the misbehaving cable had worked the family into a near frenzy.

Even though a cable TV cord offered no great haunt to discover, there was a great sense of relief for the living inhabitants of the house. As the research group points out, their work is two-fold. Sure, they'd be delighted to discover extraordinary phenomenon to study and record, but on the other hand, they also find accomplishment in helping unearth normal explanations for things. Because of this education and understanding, fear is alleviated and unnecessary actions, like packing up and moving to escape, are curtailed.

An Interview with Todd Roll
and Shawn Blaschka

What's the number one piece of advice for the wannabe ghost hunter?

Keep an open mind. Just because people truly believe that a place is haunted, does not mean that it is. In fact, the statistics of explainable phenomenon vs. unexplainable phenomenon, would tell us that it is likely *not* haunted. Some people lie. But serious clients believe what they are telling you to be true, and you must remain objective, take the information in respectfully, and at the same time, absorb it with total objectivity.

Gather and study the evidence, and don't be in a hurry to decide whether paranormal activity is taking place or not. Patience is your friend. Don't expect instant results. Use a keen eye and be observant. Listen. If you're only looking for one thing, you're going to develop tunnel vision. You don't want to go from researcher-investigator to becoming an occupant of the home, which is easy to do. Then you lose objectivity that is critical to this work.

Cats and dogs — they seem to detect things we're not seeing. What do you think they are reacting to at those times?

Animals in general have sharper senses than humans do. They can hear sounds we can't, smell things we can't, and see things we can't. But knowing what they are reacting to can be difficult to determine. It could be termites, or chipmunks in your walls; could be a high-pitched sound coming from an appliance; could be very low infra sound. Or is could be something paranormal.

Small children around one to four years' old have minds that are not so cluttered with busy thoughts. They can reflect on things that are not preconceived. One theory says that the mind only allows you to see what you can understand. Maybe this is bizarre, but in many ways, it is believable.

Shawn: I lived in a home once for six or seven years that I consider haunted, although this didn't bother us. My cat acted strange, but she was strange to begin with. It's hard to say and it's hard to prove anything paranormal was active. My youngest child would stare into the hallway and look into the other bedroom as if he were watching someone in the other room. I don't know what he was seeing that I wasn't seeing.

What information do you gather before pursuing an alleged haunt?

We ask numerous questions before we decide to investigate a place or a phenomenon. We want to gather information on the history. We want a definite description of the unusual or disturbing activity. What's been seen or heard; have there been unusual odors or scents?

We often ask people to keep a diary so we can look for patterns. What time of day is this happening? How many people live in the house? What are your [client] thoughts as to what is happening? Have you experienced anything in your sleep, and has it only been at this residence? Has there been anybody in your lineage with apparent psychic abilities?

These are some of the general questions. The questions become more specific as the investigation continues.

What finding do you think is most conclusive of a haunting, in your opinion?

Todd: My personal belief is that paranormal phenomenon is electromagnetic in nature. Therefore, if we detect a field where we normally would not expect to find a field, then that is good evidence of paranormal activity to me. A sudden temperature change or a photograph would also be good evidence.

Shawn: The voice recording is a big thing for me. I listened to the tape of the Grand Theater many times. I can't explain to you how that unfamiliar voice would show up on a tape—a new tape, fresh out of the package. There were two people in the room and there were no voices but ours in the area. The other two investigators were two floors below us, not even within earshot. The rest of the building was vacant. How is that possible that a voice out of nowhere is suddenly on my tape?

Seeing something, photographing a shape or an apparition would be strong evidence also. The jump when an electromagnetic field increases is evidential. When a ghost manifests, it seems to remove energy in the form of heat from the air. This causes a temperature drop. Some people look for change in ion count in the atmosphere. Ions attach themselves to radioactivity. Spirit activity supposedly changes the amount of ions that are active in a particular area. There's an accessible level of radioactivity on the planet, and supposedly, if a spirit is present, the radioactivity shows a rise. These are less conclusive, but they are theories that are studied.

Photographs, digital vs. photographic film—your preference?

Photographic film is best. Digital is cheap and economical and makes a good quality control, but it can't be analyzed like a film negative. Digital photos are less believable than a 35mm because they can easily be altered. Orbs seem to appear more often on digital for some reason. These bubble-like translucent objects can be caused by so many things, including moisture in the air, dust, and insects.

Movies and TV shape people's perceptions about haunting and spirit entities. For example, the public often see ghosts and "demons" as one and the same. Your comments?

Shawn: Media handling of such topics tends to frighten people unnecessarily. In my opinion, *Amityville Horror*—complete hogwash. The movie, *Poltergeist*, is a classic example of poltergeist ("noisy ghost") activity with a lot of Hollywood sensationalizing. The film was actually based on a case from a haunted location in Rothschild (Wausau area) in the 1970's.

The media likes to scare people. They like to say every ghost is evil. Sometimes people base their attitude about spirits on religious beliefs, and some of those ideas include evil entities such as a devil. Nobody has been killed by a ghost. You're more likely to fall over something and injure yourself if you're scared and running. I've never run into an "evil" situation. If you're not frightened at times, you're not alive. Sometimes, as an investigator, you feel completely freaked out. We work in groups of two for credibility and for comfort.

Todd: My belief is that the spirit does not survive death. What people see as ghosts can be explained away as a number of things such as hallucination, hoax, misinterpretation of mundane events, the replaying of a specific event in time, or perhaps a window into another dimension. Demons don't exist and have nothing to do with ghosts.

Do you know how to get rid of a ghost?

We don't do this, but we can recommend others. It depends on the person's beliefs. Sometimes people have religious beliefs that would prompt them to call a minister or priest or other religious practitioner.

What about residual haunting vs. true haunting?

A residual haunting fades over time. It is not considered a real spirit. For example, if you see the same "woman in white" figure come down the steps every night at 10PM, this is residual. It's like a movie repeating itself. On the other hand, a true haunting would have the spirit appear at random, possibly trying to communicate. Some of the castles in England are truly haunted. The ghosts don't dissipate.

What happens if a building or a house is torn down? Does the spirit remain with the property?

Shawn: That's an interesting question. I've thought about this, and it seems as though a spirit may stay at the same location and operate in a different dimension. The spirit may still be "seeing" the house it was originally associated with in life.

Have you had any cases of poltergeist ("noisy ghost") activity?

Yes, we had a case that involved slamming of cupboard doors and dishes moving from one end of the room to the other. These cases most often occur when a young woman in puberty is in the house, as it did in this case. The phenomenon seems to come on suddenly and leave almost as abruptly. In this case, the activity lessened or disappeared at times when the daughter was out of the house. Poltergeist activity is bizarre because it's thought to be a person causing the uproar, either through his or her own psychokinetic energy, or by acting as a host for spirit energy.

Todd Roll and Shawn Blaschka, lead investigators of the Wausau Paranormal Research Society, kindly gave us their time, and interviewed for this chapter. The organization has a mission to collect research and educate through their community service. They do not charge a fee. The group can be reached through their website at www.pat-wausau.org

What the Unexplained Experts Tell Us

Chad Lewis and Terry Fisk wrote a book titled *The Wisconsin Road Guide to Haunted Locations.* Who better to ask about ghosts than the "been there-done it" team?

What are the details on a case(s) that you investigated, but turned out to have a "normal" explanation? Conversely, what are the details on a case that turned out to be unexplained?

Several cases that we have investigated have turned out to have a normal explanation. However, the majority of cases that I investigate seem to linger in the realm of unexplained. They cannot easily be proved or disproved. [Note: by the time Chad and Terry are contacted, it is likely the alleged paranormal phenomenon has occurred for some time, thus, cases accepted for investigation have a greater likelihood of leaning toward the category of unexplained.]

In your opinion, where is the most haunted place in Wisconsin?

Chad Lewis: I believe the most haunted place in Wisconsin is Caryville. I don't think it is haunted for all the typical reasons. Terry Fisk and I have debunked most of the "causes" for haunting. .

If you found no paranormal activity at these places in Caryville, then why do you believe it is the most haunted place in Wisconsin?

Chad: Good question. Just because the reported history of a place is inaccurate, does not mean that paranormal activity is absent. It seems that individuals who visit Caryville with a preconceived notion that it is haunted actually have something happen to them. The much harder question arises when we look at human perception and belief systems. Here's is how I look at this case. We found no evidence of anybody hanging himself at Caryville. We found no evidence that a child died in the schoolhouse. Despite this, people are still experiencing things they believe to be paranormal in nature at Caryville. What is it about a person's makeup that allows them to "experience" the paranormal? Are these experiences based in reality? I don't know. What I do know is that these experiences are perceived real to the people experiencing them. Caryville is one of the areas that people contact Terry and me about the most. It is an extremely popular place to visit to try to experience a ghost or a haunting.

Caryville—the Investigations—the Legends

Caryville Old Cemetery is properly known as the Sand Hill Cemetery. It is located around Eau Claire in Dunn County. The investigation detected nothing out of the ordinary when using an EMF meter (electromagnetic field), IR thermo probe (infrared), photographs, and EVP (electronic voice phenomena). Legend has it that ghosts of children run in the field next to the cemetery. Some of the ghosts have approached people and spoken to them.

It is further reported that a tall, dark shadowy figure roams the graveyard. The investigators noted this could be "Blackie" the same entity reported at the Caryville schoolhouse, and the Meridean boat landing. Growling sounds emanate from the cemetery. People associate this with hellhounds. Local lore claims things happen in the cemetery after midnight, especially on Halloween, and that Ouija boards go out of control in the place. *Unsolved Mysteries* reportedly featured the graveyard on their program, and they supposedly detected ghostly activity. Some say there is a neglected and forgotten cemetery deeper in the woods where a pugilist-type entity appears, especially if the intruder spits or curses the graves.

Chad and Terry were unable to locate a remote cemetery in the woods, and the owner of the land is unaware of its existence. The investigators doubt that the cemetery was portrayed on *Unsolved Mysteries*, and as mentioned previously, the team noted nothing paranormal at the time they investigated it.

Spring Brook Lutheran Church in Caryville is allegedly haunted by a minister named "Jacob." Another version of the legend says Jacob was a priest. The story says that about thirty years ago, investors came to town and had plans to demolish the church and schoolhouse across the road. The enraged minister supposedly removed the stairs and committed suicide by hanging himself in the belfry, with the townspeople spotting him through the window later. After that, the legend of the hanging minister sprung to life.

In their investigation, Chad and Terry found that the rumors have flourished for 5-10 years, not thirty years. The story of the suicide is false. Local residents and church members have not observed paranormal activity.

Spring Brook School is located across from the church, and looks like a typical old one room schoolhouse. Legends abound. The ghostly history reports that a boy attending school died under mysterious circumstances, although this is not specific. Some say the boy refused to go home one day in January to his drunken father, hid at school, and was found the next day frozen to death in his desk. Not to be outdone with that story, another version says a preacher killed all the children, and then hanged himself in the belfry of the school.

Investigators Chad and Terry did some digging and found out that David John Grohn (1949-1957) attended the school, and died on September 24, 1957 at Luther Hospital in Eau

Claire from polio. The examining physician, Dr. C.H. Falstad, at autopsy reported nothing unexpected. Allegations of abuse by the father appear to be false, and evidence that a preacher committed murder and suicide is lacking.

So what's going on at the school? Phenomena include a pair of black eyes that stare from the last window on the right side of the building, blood spattered on the walls following the rape of a girl by a ghost inside the school, and a three-legged, one-eyed cat who guards the school and stares at intruders if they approach the school. If that's not enough, consider the reports that a rope with a noose hangs in the belfry, and "Blackie" the shadowy demon may shake your car if you are parked near the school. Blackie might be the same creature who haunts the Carryville Cemetery and the Meridean boat landing.

Related to feeling an unusual gust of air inside the school, if a visitor sits in the desk the young boy died in, the visitor will feel a strange sensation pass through his or her body.

OK. Now what do the investigators have to say? Chad and Terry say the story of the rape is unsubstantiated, and no evidence of bloodstains on the walls exists. They couldn't find the cat, and it is doubtful that anybody knows which desk the deceased boy sat in, since this was fifty years ago. Nonetheless, the investigators sat in each of the desks, and found nothing paranormal about the game of musical chairs. However, they encountered one witness who claimed seeing the noose and feeling the mysterious gust of wind inside the school.

Meridean (incorrectly referred to as "Meridian" or "Maridean") is an island on the Chippewa River (not the "Meridian River"). Chad and Terry found out there was a town named Meridean on the island during the lumbering days. Today, a boat landing has replaced a ferry crossing used to traverse the Chippewa River to the island. A number of stories as to how the island got its name have come down through the years. A commonality in the stories is that a young girl named "Mary Dean" was traveling with her mother on the Chippewa River by steamboat. The youngster won the hearts of other travelers, but became acutely ill, and was taken ashore. The illness was fatal. Mary Dean was buried near a tree on the island. The area bears the name "Meridean" in commemoration.

Again, legends abound. Stories tell us that the ghost of Mary Dean haunts the island and boat landing where she committed suicide. Another tale says that three ferries disappeared in the area, resulting in closure of the ferry crossing. Still another account claims several teenagers drowned in the area, and the deaths were a result of suicide.

Just as bizarre, is the yarn of a sanitarium that was located on the island. The institution was reportedly run by a doctor who owned several dogs, and now a pack of ghostly dogs roams the island. The black phantom dogs, known as hellhounds, have glowing red eyes. The beasts supposedly killed the child of their owner. The hellhound legend takes on a glow of it's own in the report that about 50 years ago, two kids were parked in a pickup truck at the boat landing, and attacked by animals. The abandoned truck was awash with blood splatters and unidentified animal hair. The bodies were missing.

Chad and Terry team once again brought out the magnifying glass. They were not able to find any documentation that verified disappearance of the ferries, nor could they find reports of any drowning. Local historian, Dick Feeney, noted there was never a sanitarium on the island, and reports of a doctor who ran a sanitarium and kept dogs appear to be false.

What's been happening that perpetuates the myths? Folks have reported seeing the ghost of Mary Dean near the boat landing. Probably even more disturbing is the howling and growling of the hellhounds, and the shocking stare of glowing red eyes in the woods near the boat landing. Some people even claim they've seen the hellhounds running down Caryville Road. Rumors persist of nocturnal screaming and movement in the woods in conjunction with an ominous shadowy figure darting across the road.

One eyewitness saw a bonfire and a huge statuesque chair across the road from the boat landing while three pairs of shining red eyes pierced the night in the nearby woods. It's been said that if you dare park your car near the boat landing at the bottom of the hill below the Caryville Cemetery, and shut off your headlights, the hellhounds will appear.

What do the investigators have to say? The team actually heard animal-like noises on the island, and they were not able to connect the sounds to any known species.

They interviewed the eyewitness who described the huge chair and alarming red eyes, however it is possible that the chair was actually a deer stand since the area is frequented by hunters. Bonfires in the area are common, since the Meridean boat landing and the island are popular sites for camping and teen parties, which could also account for any "screaming."

Caryville Road, otherwise known as "240th Avenue," is a place where your car headlights, taillights, and interior lights fail to function, or so the story goes. Headlights of phantom cars appear and disappear, as the cars chase and play chicken with real life drivers on the road. Your car's interior turns into a refrigerator, no matter how high you crank up the heat. And if you haven't lost your mind yet, and have the wherewithal to check your odometer, the distance from county road H to the bridge is longer than the distance from the bridge to county road H. Are you lost in a time-space gap?

How did all this come about? According to legend, many years ago, a girl was driving home after attending a prom, and was killed when her car left the road, and tumbled over the bridge. A similar version says that "Jenny," the lovely prom queen, was partying that night, lost control of her pickup truck, and a fatal accident resulted.

Local residents refute any car accident at the bridge, but if you see an old red car (or pickup truck) erratically driving down the road, it may spark your mind to recall the old tales.

Or, if you happen to glance into the water running beneath the bridge, you could be startled by the beam of eerie head-lights beneath the dark water. Okay, so there you have it. What the investigators found was that an odometer check measured the distance to and from the bridge as 1.9 miles both ways, no phantom cars or headlights were observed, and the water did not reveal any lights from the depths.

Please, if you're thinking of checking out Caryville sites, be considerate and mindful of the laws regarding trespassing. The community also has had numerous problems with vandalism. The Dunn County Sheriff's Department requests that any vandalism be reported to them at non-emergency 715-232-1564. Trespassers and those who commit vandalism will be subject to arrest and prosecution.

More questions for the investigator....

A place is rumored to be haunted, but you often have your doubts. Why?

After visiting hundreds of the most paranormal places around the world, I have yet to experience anything that I would without hesitation, classify as paranormal. Most places have so much urban legend surrounding them that when you start to investigate, the case falls apart. Again, it is important to emphasize, this does not mean it is not haunted. Yet many times, it places the sole evidence on the witnesses.

Your comments to wannabe ghost hunters...

The majority of people are not looking for the latest scientific study on the paranormal. They are looking to go on a good legend trip. With this, I recommend that they use common sense when investigating the paranormal. Have fun and enjoy these stories for what they are, and don't become disappointed if nothing happens on your trip. For the serious researcher, I recommend getting training in

other fields including the sciences, folklore, critical thinking, psychology, sociology, and so on. I also advise them to
let the evidence guide in their investigation. Do not allow
your personal beliefs to interfere with objectivity needed
to investigate a case thoroughly and accurately.

*We extend many thanks to Chad Lewis, paranormal
researcher, for contributing to this essay. For more information on Chad Lewis, Terry Fisk, and their radio broadcast,
check out www.unexplained.com and The Wisconsin Road
Guide to Haunted Locations (2004 Unexplained Research
Publishing Company) by Chad Lewis and Terry Fisk.*

**With its cemetery, church and
schoolhouse, Caryville, near Eau
Claire, may be the most haunted
place in Wisconsin.**

Files of the Southern Wisconsin Paranormal Research Group

We had an interesting conversation with Jennifer Lauer, founder of the Southern Wisconsin Paranormal Research Group. David Schumacher contributed to this interview. Here's what they had to say:

Describe your most unusual or baffling Wisconsin case.

We've encountered several intriguing cases, but most recently, we investigated the *Bar Next Door* in Madison. The case is actually ongoing, but our first visit was spectacular—just amazing. The bar is comprised of a first floor, second floor, and basement. At one time, it was a speakeasy known as the Wonder Bar. Our team was not told a lot about the place before we entered into the investigation. Basically, we were told that strange occurrences were happening and the staff wanted us to check it out for them.

We set up equipment on all three floors. The first floor is a bar area and the second floor is a meeting room-pool-room-gathering place. We were taking usual readings on our equipment when the equipment in the upstairs and basement simultaneously went crazy. It's the best way I can describe it, short of giving you the technicalities of what was coming down.

We had still-frame motion detection cameras in the basement, which takes shots when there is any movement. Nobody was in that basement when our equipment upstairs recorded significant changes. About 2 seconds later, the cameras in the basement jumped into action and recorded shots. It's as if something went through the entire building. We caught three frames of a ball of light, and the speed was detected at 60-80 miles per hour. We have an event called Dining with the Dead, where we'll be returning to the Bar Next Door, explaining what happened, and checking things out again.

We found out later that the rumor is there's a body buried behind the upstairs fireplace. It would certainly be interesting to know if that's true, but we won't be busting open the fireplace—probably a good idea to let the mystery be what it is.

Another great place we investigated was the Brumder Mansion Bed and Breakfast in Milwaukee. There is especially a lot of activity in the bathroom. One of our investigators was in the bathroom and somebody was jiggling the door handle. He came downstairs and said, "OK you guys, knock it off." Nobody was up there.

We'd like to investigate the Spaulding House Antique Shop again in Janesville. We investigated it in 2003 after receiving many reports of strange occurrences, so many that the employees began keeping a journal of them. For example, a woman in 1800's clothing was seen walking into the green room upstairs. The aroma of freshly baked bread came from what formerly was the kitchen. The heat was repeatedly turned up in the ladies' room. When employees closed up for the night and shut the lights off, they'd turn back to look at the house, and the lights upstairs would be on again. There have been so many instances of paranormal activity in that establishment.

Describe a case where people were frightened and convinced that a haunting was occurring, but you found out differently.

A case in Iowa is important to bring up as an example

that brings with it a caveat. All right, we'll take a break from Wisconsin for a moment here. The Villisca Axe Murder House case is difficult to talk about because it is so horrific. The murders occurred in Villisca, Iowa. In the house of J.B. Moore in the early 1900's, five children and two adults were murdered in their beds as they slept. The current owners of the house invited different groups to investigate the place. So we went, and investigated it as thoroughly as possible. We came up with very little that we'd consider paranormal activity. When we gave the owners the report, they became angry. They posted nasty things about the group, said we were just taking pictures, didn't know what we were talking about, and so on.

The story behind the story was that the show *Proof Positive*, a Sci-Fi channel feature was coming to check out the place. This particular show likes things black and white—in other words, they want to absolutely prove or absolutely disprove. The house was going to be on the show—to prove or disprove that the property was haunted. The owners or caretakers of the house said that we'd be sorry and look foolish because the show was certainly going to prove the place haunted. We thought…well, OK…whatever…fine, but we still could not say that we had found anything we would consider significant. It was constant bickering with these people. We just wanted them to drop it. Sorry we didn't find anything, but that's the way it is.

Proof Positive came to Villisca, Iowa and got the same results. They too could not claim that they had found anything noteworthy enough to proclaim the place haunted.

Then the owners got extremely angry with us and began giving us even more grief, saying we must have had a hand in the show's decision. It is a case of a person who had an old house with a history, who wanted to make a buck. There are many places that we have not been able to catch evidence leaning either way. Just as in other areas of life, when you go out to investigate things, there's a right time and place, and you may just be at a location at a time when nothing is happening. The results are inconclusive, and it is common to return to a place two or three times to continue testing.

What's your advice to the wannabe paranormal investigator?

Keep a level head. Don't sway too much one way or the other. Use as much scientific base as possible, and document and back up everything that you do. As investigators, our goal is to have science recognize this as a science, and to be put into a category. In established scientific research, you have to take something into the lab and replicate your results over and over in order to come up with any conclusion. With this stuff, that's hard to do. We want to show that we use science as a foundation, and that we do have hard evidence for what we are trying to prove or disprove. With this kind of evidence, the public will take us more seriously. Try to prove any natural occurrence before you conclude that something is unnatural or supernatural.

How about cats and dogs? Are they ahead of the game in detecting things?

It's hard to say what they react to; they see in a different spectrum than we do. We think animals can see in the infrared spectrum. In the process of investigation, we have been able to capture phenomena on infrared (IR). If it's true that something is in the IR spectrum, than it would make sense that animals can see it and react to it, whereas humans do not experience it, simply because IR is out of range for humans. Our research group has actually had several experiences surrounding this. One interesting case is at the Brumder Mansion in Milwaukee. The owner said she would not allow dogs up in Aunt Pussy's room. This Auntie allegedly haunts the Brumder Mansion. The ghost does not like animals, particularly dogs. If dogs enter Aunt Pussy's room, abnormal things start happening around the house, and the owner is afraid that harm will come to any dogs there. The dogs bark for no reason and chase things that aren't visibly seen by human eyes.

What measure do you find is the most conclusive for ghostly paranormal activity?

It's not one specific thing; it's a variety of things correlating and happening at around the same time. The atmosphere has changed and something has gone through the atmosphere to make it change. What the change is, we don't know. It could be paranormal, or for that matter, it could be normal. We don't know. Maybe it's a solar flare. If we capture something at the same time—if it moves, or you capture audio and video, at the same time that EMF (electromagnetic field) and thermal scanner respond, then we will say that there is some other force in this room. We don't know if it the energy of someone who has died or not. All we know is that something is in the room that wasn't there five minutes ago.

People assume this is due to a ghost. We can't assume this. If you define a haunting as these elements fitting together, then yes, I would guess by definition, you have a haunting. We rarely say something is haunted. I've said the Spaulding House Antique shop in Janesville is haunted. Something happened to me there. A disembodied voice of a woman told me to go away. The owner was standing with me at the time, and we both heard it. I have no other documentation other than to say something weird happened to me that I can't explain.

Is there a fear factor for you?

I'm more afraid of the living. I've never been harmed or threatened by anything I can't see. Sometimes you get the chill up your back—a cold draft that goes up your back and into your neck. But I think that's some kind of natural response not necessarily related to fear. I've been in abandoned prisons and mental hospitals, homes, basements—you name it, but

I've never been afraid. As a paranormal investigator, I think I am of a "charged" mind that says, "Yah great. Now, did I catch that on audio?" That's when you turn into high gear. Something is happening, and we can document it. I used to be afraid of the paranormal; it's a fear of the unknown, but now I understand it more.

Media damage? What's your opinion on how the media shapes perception?

The media shapes people's perceptions big time. In the course of this, we get entertainment. We were conditioned to be frightened and audiences expect to be frightened through the media. However, being an investigator is actually boring. Imagine just watching, waiting, checking meters, and then finding little to no activity—that's pretty unexciting. It really lacks the entertainment component. We've had several requests for people who want to go along on an investigation, and we don't accommodate that. For one thing, there's a confidentiality factor. Secondly, their expectations are tied to the media, and in real life, this kind of sensationalism doesn't happen. The media does a lot of damage, and consequently it's difficult to be taken seriously in this field. Nonetheless, I have fun and I love it.

Some groups do this purely for the entertainment value. They go to cemeteries and take photos, looking for orbs or other phenomena. That's known as "ghost hunting," which is on the lower end of the spectrum. The polar opposite is parapsychology. Degree programs in several universities exist for parapsychology, which is the scientific study of psychic phenomenon. We're in the middle some place—a mixture of ghost hunting and parapsychology. When we do our outings, which are activity boosters for the organization, I always call them ghost hunts because they're fun, and that's the most accurate description of them. When we do an actual investigation, that's when we really get down to work; collect readings, and so on. The movie *Ghost Busters* alludes to methods that are based on factual methods of investigation. Basically, they are trying to detect changes in the atmosphere. I love that movie.

What events do you find strongly relate to a haunting?

It depends on the type of haunting. Three types exist. In what's known as *intelligent haunting*, the ghost interacts with you, probably scares you, and is a human- like. This is the rarest haunting, and is spectacular. In a *residual haunting*, the walls or the area has captured some kind of energy, and the energy is released periodically. Things are replayed like an old movie. These are the kinds of situations where you might see the "ghost" walking down the hallway or down the stairs. This is the most common event, has nothing to do with someone who has died, and is a moment in time being replayed.

The third type of haunting has to do with *poltergeist activity* due to a human agent. Often, but not exclusively, this comes from a young female between the ages of twelve to twenty years old who is going through stressful times. Apparently, the energy in the brain misfires, and the energy is directed outward. Things break, windows open and shut, fires start. She is not aware that she is doing this. It settles down, however. The best way to determine whether this is poltergeist activity is to remove the person from the house and see if the activity continues. Sometimes medical or psychiatric attention can help alleviate the stress, and get rid of the "ghost."

The greatest places to see a haunting—*residual haunting* usually—would be in places where there's been people connection—theaters, hospitals, arenas, hallways, staircases. Sometimes they are places that are associated with emotions, as in a theater where there's laughing, crying, and intense moments.

Do you think it's possible for objects such as jewelry to be haunted?

I suppose it's possible, but I've never encountered this. As far as somebody claiming an object is haunted and the person is trying to sell it to you, I'd say don't waste your money.

Weird Wisconsin quips and comments

Summer is in the air as we write this, and the authors of *Weird Wisconsin*, Linda Godfrey and Richard Hendricks, have completed their travels to far corners of the state—at least for now. We spoke with author Linda Godfrey about paranormal investigation. Here's what the sleuth had to say...

An Interview with Linda Godfrey

What tools do you use for objective research, and what do you rely on subjectively?

I really like to read old newspapers, books, and documents. When I hear a story, what I like to do is find out the particulars. Has a person matching the description of the alleged ghost ever lived or died in that house? There's no objective proof of a ghost. What's the history of the area? Look at maps, and interview various people. The curious investigators with a scientific bend use electronic equipment and cameras to try collecting evidence. I have equipment, but I tend to use these other means. Also, I don't have much luck getting orbs in my photos. Orbs don't actually prove anything, other than they might just be another interesting piece of the puzzle. What I do is look for are tales about encounters with these strange entities. That can tell a lot. Interactions, descriptions, and multiple people experiencing the event, are factors necessary to research. Dive into the history as far back as possible. Every case is different.

In your work, do people come to you, or are you actively out there searching on your own?

For the book *Weird Wisconsin,* I was out there actively searching. Some things just occur as a result of searching for other things. For example, I had gone to Sparta to look into a place, and was asking directions when a person said to me, "Did you know we have a haunted soap store?" So of course, I ran and immediately went to the haunted soap store. People do come to me much of the time, even though I am better known for wolf man, dog man and strange creatures. But people weave ghost encounters, UFO's, and all kinds of strange things into that. They'll often tell me their house is haunted, or inform me about all kinds of bizarre experiences.

I've had folks show me strange scars on their bodies that they claim are made by ghosts or little people in their houses. One woman had a diagram of where aliens had cut away part of her body when she was abducted. It pretty much runs the gamut. If I'm not into a book or something where I have to be focusing so much on one thing, I do like to follow up on these stories.

Pertaining to ghosts, what do you think is your most baffling case?

I think the story in the *Weird Wisconsin* book about one of the nursing home care facilities in Lacrosse is quite strange. A trustworthy individual volunteered the story to me and I interviewed the person who works at the location. All the nurses and personnel at the care facility know about it, but none of the staff has seen this apparition. A few days before a number of deaths, the dementia patients, or a patient who is very ill and near death, will see the ghost of a little boy. The residents of the home try to follow him out of the room. They become concerned, and want to find the boy to take care of him, thinking he's one of their children, and things like that. He's often seen wearing a baseball cap and carrying a cat.

When the staff starts getting these messages of a little boy sighting, they start preparing, because they know there's going to be a cluster of deaths happening soon. No known history of a boy dying on the property exists, and children have not been housed at this care facility. The nursing home staff don't know if the child is there as an escort, or a warning, or a spiritual comforter for these people or what. The history of the property is unremarkable.

Pertaining to any investigation, what prompts you to want to investigate these phenomenons?

Curiosity, as you said, and I've always been interested in things unexplainable. Growing up, I loved fairy tale books. My dad had science fiction books around, so I had that curiosity about aliens and other worlds. I liked to hear ghost stories. It just sticks with you. I was raised in a church-going Lutheran family, and I had many questions the minister couldn't, or didn't, want to explain. This befuddlement spurred me to go out on my own in search of answers. ESP, ghosts, aliens—do they really exist? I started investigating things really in my early 20's. I had two rules—no séances and no Ouija boards.

I had bad experiences with séances in the dorm at Whitewater. I lived in Wells Hall, which was always rumored to be haunted anyhow. I had a dormitory acquaintance who conducted séances. After a troubling incident, I spent the rest of the semester having to sleep with the lights on, much to the dismay of the roommate. Staying away from séances and Ouija, I still found a lot to investigate.

How did you first stumble upon Beast of Bray Road?

The Beast of Bray Road was a completely different thing. I had never paid much attention to the subject of werewolves, but I just really love the mystery. I was working as a columnist and cartoonist for *The Week*, which is a Walworth County newspaper based in Delevan. One of the freelancers tipped me off that people were reporting a creature that looked like a werewolf to the county animal control officer. When I checked around town, I found out that was true. And I also found out that the animal control officer had a manila folder labeled "Werewolf." At this point, it became news. Nobody else really wanted to touch it, but it was a slow news time, and the editor and I agreed it would be a fun story to run for a couple of weeks. People would get a few chuckles out of it.

Little did we know it would be picked up by Associated Press nationally and internationally. Within weeks, I was simply besieged by radio and TV from all over the country. *Inside Edition* came out and did a half hour story. It was just wild. That made me "Werewolf Central." Suddenly I became the expert, like it or not. I had to go through a learning curve actually to bone up on all of the lore. People would come to me with questions, and I wanted to know the answers myself. But also, people contacted me whenever they saw something like this. The spotting of a wolf man or a dog man or other type of extraordinary creature started being referred to me. I began this strange collection of stories. I never imagined it would mushroom into what it has. People would ask me, is this going to be a book or a career, and I'd say, "Oh, I don't think so." But after ten years, I really did have enough material. All the things I had collected, experiences, and theories added up.

Actually, I had published a different book first, *The Poison Widow*, which was a story related to more research I had done while working on the newspaper. After Trails put that out, they said, "What else do you have?" I said, "Werewolf?" Once they understood how much folklore and local history was involved, they were enthusiastic about the project. The book has done well, and I'm working on the sequel.

I've been on eight or nine national TV shows and Canada's Global TV Network. They've all come to me and found me. I think that's because this is a unique phenomenon. There have been so many contemporary sightings of what appears to be a wolf man or dog man. I hate to use "werewolf" because that gives a connotation that there is a human being doing the Lon Cheney thing, but I don't know that's the case here. I'm up to more than fifty incidents reported. The only thing I can compare it to would be the "Moth man," a creature spotted around West Virginia most recently.

What's an important message for wannabe investigators?

Very important—do not trespass on private property. That's what gets numerous people in trouble. Secondly, don't expect you can go to a site where something has happened and experience the same thing. Everybody goes to Bray Road. I don't know of a single person who has gone there hoping to see the Beast of Bray Road, and managed to do so. The sightings has spread all over the state now, but the creature has not been seen on Bray Road for years and years. That's where people go because it's in the title of a book.

People will know of a certain type of ghost at a specific house, and will go there expecting to see the same. That rarely happens. Sometimes readings will be picked up, however. A few of the people that I know who have done this a lot, will detect voices, but it really is quite rare. It's a lot of sitting around, watching, waiting, doing boring activities. With the most recent wolf man sighting, we were able to set up a nighttime stakeout. I knew the people who owned the land, and we had permission to do this. I had handpicked a team. We had cameras, walkie-talkies, and other equipment; we roamed this place until the wee hours of the morning and came up with nothing. That didn't surprise any of us.

Learn to record a lot and take detailed notes. Atmospheric conditions, the date, the weather, notes of what people are talking about, even though it may sound minor at the time, can all become significant. Carry a ruler too. If you take a photo, you want to have a reference point. You might put the ruler, a coin, or some common reference in the photo itself. Objectify the size of the footprint or handprint, and so on, by using the ruler in the photo.

Do you need to go into this with a certain kind of mindset?

You have to be patient. Avoid being extremely negative and avoid being overly hopeful. Try to remain neutral or you're likely to read too much into it. If you pooh-pooh things, you'll shut yourself off from things that you might otherwise perceive.

Is there a fear factor for you?

People always say, "Aren't you scared to go out hunting for the werewolf." At times, I've been nervous about maybe having to confront an animal like a bear or wild dog. Rick and I spent hours last summer trudging around a northern pine meadow looking for the remains of a ghost town. When you think about it, bears or mountain lions could have been in the area. I am more afraid of the living flesh and blood beings—four legged and two legged. As far as the Beast of Bray Road, there has never been a report of a single scratch on a human being. It seems only to want to get away.

As far as ghosts, some people have a fear that the ghost will follow them home, or that ghosts are demons. I actually saw an apparition in the haunted soap maker's store in Sparta that I mentioned earlier. This was a rare event for me. The apparition appeared in a short white painted hallway, which is an area between the store and the basement. The tombstone of Christiane Strommen is in the stone basement wall of the store. The owner's husband has seen the apparition in that area several times. I walked through the hallway, and for some reason, I turned around and looked back. I saw this apparition resembling a floating torso. It was the approximate shape and size of a human torso that was white and gray, and was floating about the right height from the floor. I couldn't see where a reflection was coming in or anything like that.

Immediately my reporter mind was saying, "Okay, where's that coming from?" I couldn't answer it. Then it faded away. I wasn't afraid of what I was seeing, but maybe if it were night time or I was alone, things would have been different. So, did I have a camera? Yes, I did, but I was too flabbergasted to use it! I took a picture after it faded, but nothing showed up. There is a lot of activity in the place, however.

Many men who are outdoorsmen and hunters, as well as women and children, who have seen the wolf man or dog man were scared to pieces. Some who have observed it at a distance say it is disturbing, and they think about it every day to try to figure out what it is. The memory haunts them.

What events do you think are most closely related to haunting?

A common denominator is the attachment either to material things, or to the place of habitation. It seems that when people are recording personality ghosts, sometimes there is a trauma. Yet others, whose ghost appears, have died peacefully and they don't want to give the place up. Perhaps some are materialistic and don't want to give up the things they had in life. Even trauma can be viewed as an attachment. There's no way to prove this, but you can understand that a person would want to stay anchored to a spot.

Do you think ghosts travel? Would I be bringing one home with me?

I think that if we're talking about something living in the

gauge is used because some manifestations are vaporous, and this helps us determine if the vapor is natural or paranormal. Four members of our team are intuitive, and we rely on them for clairvoyance, sensitivity, and so on. All members of the team document and record anything they have seen, heard, sensed, and so on. We do this separately and then draw a conclusion from all of our data.

Pertaining to ghosts, describe your most unexplainable and baffling case.

We've had a few baffling cases, but I think the most remarkable is one we investigated in Kenosha, Wisconsin. A large family was dealing with multiple occurrences. The many witnesses included every member of the family, friends, family members who did not reside in the home, and even appliance repair men. I did considerable research on the home, and did not discover anything that would show classic tales of why the haunting would occur. The symptoms of the haunting included dark shadows, billows of rotating black and white smoke that materialized, a girl who levitated from the futon, and people being physically harmed in all areas of the house. Other bizarre things include "notes" that the family swears was from the spirit. Kids in the house used an Ouija board after they already felt there was a presence in the house.

Much of our equipment malfunctioned while investigating this house. One member of the team felt as if he were being held down with pressure while sitting in a chair. Video footage and EVP (electronic voice phenomenon) indicated there was a presence there at the time. Another member of the team mentioned that she felt the place was an old mortuary or funeral home. More research showed that for a period of three years, it was a morgue in the early 1900's. Following that, it became a home for the physically and mentally disabled. There is no record of any unnatural deaths occurring.

Months after this investigation, the family reported that all had been quiet for the most part.

What prompts you to want to investigate these phenomena?

What prompts me is the desire to help people, as I was unable to be helped once. I want their fear and disturbances to stop. The worst of fears is something invisible or something unpredictable. I strive to explain the truths versus the myths in this field. This kind of phenomena is more common than people realize. I feel a need to educate people on what a ghost or a haunting is, and to counsel them on what they can do to prevent further problems. Most of all, getting rid of whatever is present is a high priority.

Establishing proof of the existence of ghosts is not a priority. Finding evidence of an entity or a haunting in a home we are investigating is a goal, but we're mostly concerned about the client. We hope to gain insight to use in further study, to find commonalities, traits, and so on to add to what others in the field are finding. I have to admit, however, when we get some wild anomaly, or shadow, or a clear EVP, then that is very exciting!

How did this all start for you?

The paranormal has been a parallel in my life for as long as I can remember. People want answers. I rather enjoy the many unknowns. Not everything has an answer, so we have curiosity. If we lose curiosity, we lose dreams, hopes, and life. When I was thirty years old, I live in a haunted house. There were several witnesses to the events in that house. I sought help mainly because of my eight-year-old son. I sought help and contacted an investigating group. They concluded there was a presence in the house, possibly two or more entities. The group gave me some tips on what to do to rid the place of the disturbances. I was really looking for a resolution—for things to stop.

What's an important message for the wannabe investigator?

Leave your expectations at home. There are no absolutes. Be clear-minded and objective, but don't lose sight that we are spiritual beings—this must be applied to the field. We can't know everything, but it is surely fun trying! So have fun, take the work seriously, never overlook anything, never discount anything, and never draw early conclusions. Understand that research is time consuming, but valuable and essential. Do the research before entering into any investigation.

Never go into an investigation alone. There are dangers in this as far as safety is concerned, but also as far as the spiritual realm is concerned. Know your fellow investigators well enough to have trust and sense predictability. Unity and reliance is important for an investigative team. Back up your intuition with equipment and vice versa. Document! Don't believe in everything you read, see, and hear. Word of mouth is a good source of tips and hints. Be choosy about information so that you can avoid any erroneous information. Avoid misrepresenting yourself. Know your legal and moral limits. And, by all means, stock up on batteries.

Is there a fear factor for you?

Yes, I have a slight fear factor. If there weren't a fear factor, that would show ignorance, in my opinion. Fear keeps you prepared; it enables you to have your guard up.

This kind of work is not like walking into a store or a restaurant where it's likely that nothing out of the ordinary will happen. When dealing with the paranormal, I think you have to be on guard. On the other hand, I don't worry much about my safety because time and experience has prepared me for most situations. And, I trust my team. I have a fear of the spiritual aspects—that's something we can't fix with a screwdriver or heal with a band-aid. When dealing with the supernatural, one is always walking into supernatural territory, and the harms are supernatural as well.

What events do you think are most closely related to haunting?

I believe haunting is closely related to oppression and possibly even possession by supernatural forces. Some cases seem to be associated with the occult, use of the Ouija board, and spells, rituals, or a particular belief system. We continue to study this. The next event related to a haunting would be sudden deaths, whether or not traumatic.

Do you think objects, such as jewelry, can become "haunted?"

I don't believe objects can be haunted. I feel that people can give something energy, whether it be a necklace or a dresser. We give the object credence, and the objects become the target for forces to "toy" with us. If a person feels strongly that a doll is inhabited by a little girl, the person might begin to talk to the doll, give it attention, and have feelings for it. Perhaps there are forces that encourage the belief that it is haunted. Is it an attempt to manipulate the person and take the energy we give to it?

What finding or evidence is the most conclusive of a haunting?

One thing in particular is not a key to any proof. But an array of evidence that backs the data can be conclusive for us. Video footage is always exciting, but audio that can be filtered and run through software to rule out things is what our team feels is the best evidence. There are so many things to rule out. Investigators must make sure they have eliminated all practical explanations. For example, a member says that he or she saw a white sneaker walk by. Then when we get home and find that we have captured a prominent apparition of a white shoe "coming out of the wall," and we simultaneously have audio of walking in a hall. Can we chalk that all up to coincidence? Add to that high EMF readings, and temperature drops. Now, how should we view that coincidence?

The public often see ghosts and "demons" as the same because of media portrayal. Comments?

A bump in the night is not always a ghost. A ghost is not always a demon. But sometimes I feel there is a fine line between the two. I think the public is now more open than ever to the notion of ghosts, spirits, angels, and so on. In fact, they want it, and think that every dust particle in a photo is an orb, and that every coincidence is a result of divine intervention. Not so, nonetheless, people seek spirituality.

Because of movies, people see demons as red beings with horns, or zombie-like creatures who inhabit bodies, spit green vomit, and defy reality by turning our heads completely around. I believe demonic forces are real, and so are the spirits of people who have passed. Each has certain characteristics. But one does not mean the other. Our team believes it has encountered both. The public tends to believe anything they see or hear on television, and we often find ourselves "deprogramming" them.

On the topic of demons, perhaps certain souls can be used by demonic forces, but not actually exist as that specific demon. They do not "haunt" per say. They torment and torture in physical and emotional aspects. Trust me, if you're being "haunted" by a demon, you'll know it.

Do you think a spirit entity can follow a person home? Do you believe a spirit can possess somebody?

Yes. I wasn't sure of this, but my personal experience has impelled me to believe that possession is possible. We investigated a home in Milwaukee, and when we arrived at the home, I began feeling "detached." I walked off by myself, breaking our number one rule, which is to be with another person at all times. I was irritated with members, bored with the clients, and unimpressed with the entire case. I became physically hot and my ears were ringing. Something wasn't right.

My husband began to say a prayer for protection for our group, using the Bible for support. I began laughing at my husband in a mocking tone. I had the odd feeling that I was "caught" and laughing so hard, that it was almost manic. I wanted help, and began to cry uncontrollably. I was angry and cursing. "We have a problem here," was all I could manage to say. The group and I had never encountered anything like this, and they began praying over me. After about twenty minutes of prayer, I seemed to be rid of whatever the problem was. Something similar happened to the man who lived in the house.

I can't say for sure what happened. Perhaps I was what one would call "possessed?" We call it "attached to." It was a horrifying experience, and I'll never forget it. As far as entities following someone home, I do not believe ghosts have the power to travel from one place to another. I feel they are weak and remain where they are. Why they are there, we don't always know.

Heidi Linden is founder and director of Spiritual Reality Investigators (SRI). "We are much like paranormal investigators, but we deal with the spiritual and realistic aspects of the paranormal. We are Christian-based, and perform cleansings of people and homes. Our organization is non-profit, and we do not charge for our services." The group is based in Racine, Wisconsin. http://www.srealities.com

New Group
Takes a S.P.I.N.

An interview with Amy Tomlin

We decided to do just one more interview with people who dare to peer into paranormal places. Amy Tomlin of S.P.I.N., more formally known as the Stateline Paranormal Investigative Network of Wisconsin gave us a couple of strange cases. Of course, when dealing with the paranormal, the word "strange" is a run-of-the-mill claim.

S.P.I.N. is a relatively new organization composed of people who are seasoned in their paranormal investigative work. The youngest group member is Macey, age 15 who, according to her mother Amy, is quite sophisticated in her knowledge and familiarity with paranormal phenomenon.

Amy, as one of the founders of the group, emphasizes that the organization is not out to prove or disprove anything, and likens this to walking on a tight rope. The group is located in Janesville. They recently investigated a building in Monroe, Wisconsin that started out as a funeral home, and later became a private residence. The building was owned by the Stuessy family, and was constructed around 1924. It has three levels, which include a basement.

So, what was going on with the place that gave them the idea to check it all out?

The most recent residents stayed in the place from September of 2004 to March of 2005, and then felt compelled to leave because of the unexplained phenomenon and environment in general. "We'd get this feeling of emptiness and losing all heart. You felt so stagnant and like an empty shell." The residents reported lights in the kitchen going on and off, cold spots, and what they thought was a male presence throughout the house.

"We started to call it Amityville II because the moment we'd walk in the door, we'd just turn on each other, and completely irrational thoughts started coming out."

Amy, what do you make of that?

If you go into an establishment where knowingly those things have happened, it could be paranormal, but you have to put a skeptical hat on your head. We didn't pick up anything on video. One of the members, Vicky, photographed an energy vortex in the attic near some cabinets. I took a photo and caught three pink lights in the same spot. But guess what, when I took them home and examined the photos on my computer, the pink lights turned out to be car taillights shinning through a tiny window—hardly a paranormal discovery. However, in this particular case, we picked up somewhere around 50 EVPs (electronic voice phenomenon). I've analyzed all of those and noted the areas where they were picked up. The EVPs come from around areas where the owner felt the strongest presence of a male. Some of the EVPs had a malevolent character to them.

What did these voices say?

When I'm in a place, I say a little prayer and say I'm not here to harm you. The first thing that was said in this EVP recording was (male voice), "Oh God they spoke to me." Upstairs in the living quarters I was recording and still felt the male presence. I made the statement that I hoped he was at peace now. The EVP came through clearly, and said, "I am in peace." I was thinking about putting that particular EVP up on the web site.

Doesn't that scare you?

I'm so aware what EVPs are now, and I've done a lot of research. So, they don't frighten me now. Maybe people are more aware of the phenomenon because of the movie *White Noise*. Personally, I thought the movie was not very good. Getting back to the investigation of this house, I was coming down the stairs from the upper level along with the owner, and we were joking around a bit. I had my tape recorder on as usual, and was able to pick up a little girl's voice that said, "You're mean." When I first started the recordings in this place, a young girl's voice said, "They chained us." She sounded annoyed. I don't know what "they chained us" means. Another voice we got upstairs was that of a woman who kept saying "Benji." In 28 seconds of an EVP, she and a male voice said "Benji" five times. Then the man says, "Get a towel," and the woman says "Tom."

What is your explanation for an EVP?

I honestly don't know. It would be great if parapsychologists would take a closer look at this. The thing that's really strange for me is that I seem to get answers to my questions or comments. "They" are answering questions not only to me, but to other people. You might say that the phenomenon is due to radio frequencies, but tests have been done in rooms specifically designed to block out radio interference. So there is some study on this, but I'd like to see more.

You can't hear these voices unless they are on tape; right?

Right. Tthere are different classes to EVP, classes A, B, C. In one of the classes, you have to be sitting at a computer and have headphones on in order to hear. The best of course, can be picked up on a regular audio tape. I have a great EVP of a little boy singing, "pick up pickles." It's clear as a bell, and I have it on the website. It is just amazing. Some are a little whispery, so it might be difficult. EVPs used to scare me, and when you do get scary ones you have to walk away.

Do you think there are spirits or entities that are threatening and act on the threats?

I think that sometimes poltergeist activity can be that way with an adolescent in the house. I don't believe in possession. A case we had may have involved activity, but I couldn't classify it as poltergeist. The client's son had "seen a man" and supposedly, strange things were happening, but for us it was more a matter of talking the client out of it, because there didn't seem to be much weight to the claims. The child was very young. I just didn't think anything was happening there. I am a skeptic, but I do think there is something happening around us. Perhaps we live with another dimension or plane of existence, but certainly, not as we know it. If we knew all the answers, there would be no point in investigating.

From the Mysterious Journal of a Private Investigator

Sherlock Holmes in an electronic age is alive, well, and living in Wisconsin. We drove up to the house in our dark and scary midnight black-mobile on a dark and stormy night to hear his latest tales of intrigue of the person we'll call Mr. X. In real life, Mr. X is a Licensed Private Detective with all the bells and whistles, so to speak. But a most useful tool for Detective X is his prodigious psychic ability. So what is his relationship to ghosts, and why is he in this book? Indeed, this is a good question.

From an investigative viewpoint, whether you're studying paranormal entities or the hybridization of raspberries, objective science is critical, but that doesn't account for the untainted ability of the *mind*. We truly wanted to include the blended aspect of psyche and formal investigation in our book, because the composite is repeatedly and mistakenly overlooked, underestimated, or just plain thrown out with the trash. But as you will see, the alchemist really can create the gold. Please note that places, names, and a few identifying items in the following cases have been changed to protect privacy.

First, the private detective speaks...

I love solving puzzles; it's as simple as that. Mostly I work on public contracts as a private investigator. But let me backtrack here. My grandmother was a Tarot reader, and she taught me a lot when I was very young, although I think she was a joke to my mother. Nonetheless, I did readings to get through college and help pay student loans. Yes, I did make money. People said I was good, right on, and things like that, but really, I was coming from the stance of a carnival barker.

At one point, I ended up working for the Federal Reserve in transporting money, which is where I received my first serious injury when an attempt was made on my life. My position was as an investigator whose job was to pinpoint employees ripping off specific trucks. I knew how they were doing it and the logistics of it, but there was no pattern. They would steal money that was going out of circulation just when they needed some money. One day I was fueling up a truck and another truck came deliberately speeding towards me. I was hit hard by the armored truck and ended up with 118 stitches in my head, not to mention brain trauma. For months, I saw things, heard things, smelled things; stuff would jump out of the woodwork at me. I thought I was losing my mind. It took a good year to come back.

I think that a weird, and at times, harrowing upbringing, coupled with substantial injury gave me certain sensitivity to things around me. Accustomed to using Tarot cards, I started coming up with the same "information" *without* the cards. I'd have strange responses to things at work that were getting me into trouble. It came on gradually and disturbingly. Eventually, I learned to harness this ability, or harness whatever it was. I had to; I was stuck with it! For a time, large discount stores hired me to spot shoplifters. It was easy, because I was experiencing and knowing things that I didn't want to know, you might say. I'd nail a few people every day for the stores, and then take the rest of the day off.

When I worked with the Public Defender's office, things really heated up. I ended up working a lot of defense cases where you pretty much knew the guy was full of crap. I *knew* how the guy committed the crime, I'd explain it to him, he'd be all shocked, and then I'd have him sign the form; the attorney loved it. You'd get your money, the attorney would get his from the State, and the criminal would go up the river, which is where he'd actually belong.

However, there were cases, where the guy was innocent, but unfortunately he was annoying someone in the county who had the power to make things difficult. One such case is that of the mom and the motorcycle.

The case of the motorcycle and the anxious spirit

M.K. is still trying to recoup his life; I don't know if he ever will. He grew up in a medium-size city in south central Wisconsin. The county has an old west attitude, with its mining and all. M.K. was known for a rather innocuous, but rowdy drinking life style. Basically, he was a pain in the butt to the local authorities, but life went on as status quo for the most part. Then, a life-changing event started when M.K. had an argument with his common-law wife-girlfriend. She was on her way to Summer Fest but the two opted to go out on a drinking spree with a fellow motorcyclist. M.K. befriended a young woman and all three of them commenced to riding and playing "chicken" with the cycles.   The friend was a little drunk and a little high and most importantly, had little judgment. He chased down the cycle that M.K. and the woman were ridding, and tapped the back wheel of their motorcycle. Things went horribly wrong and an accident occurred. The young woman and M.K.'s friend did not survive the accident. M.K. was alive and now the owner of weighty charges filed by the District Attorney.

The minute I looked at those papers, read the report, I knew there was something other than just the story—an injustice and something far deeper. I could literally feel anger and frustration that did not belong to me. And I'm a frustrated guy to begin with! I went to the crime scene; they called it a murder scene. Actually, they called it a homicide by motor vehicle vs. a vehicular homicide, which carries a higher charge. It doesn't matter; the D.A. wanted to put this guy away.

This is where my problems began. I couldn't sleep, every physical problem I ever had got worse, and the now-deceased woman would not leave me alone. Anything I was having problems with—multiply it by 200. It was verbalizations, it was reminders left for me, and it was just everyday things in my possession, which caused me to think about this case. There seemed to be urgency, as if she were running out of time. There was anger, passion, and drama. The feelings increased when I was around the children.

M.K. was going to lose the children and I could feel that the woman did not want him to lose them. The relatives of the woman wanted the children to be "institutionalized" into foster care. Two counties were involved in the case. A forensic exam of the motorcycles was needed, but the counties didn't want to spend the money. I was about ready to give up on this case, but she would not leave me alone. This case was horrible.

The "ghost" or departed woman, however you want to refer to her, kept giving me information. I never saw her, but I heard her. She desperately kept saying it was the rock. The auditory was just clear as hell. The D.A. believed that a part of the motorcycle hit the woman on the head; and that the cycle is what killed her, after which she hit the road. This is how they accounted for the road rash on her head. *Not true.* What really happened was that she flew and hit a piece of concrete that had been pushed away from the road when the road buckles from heat and cold, and this was "the rock." Had this rock not been there, the woman would have survived the accident.

The spirit would show me her hands in a locking position with each other. I'd see this locking symbol all over the place. It was driving me nuts and it literally hurt. I threw things, acted out of character, got fired from an attorney's office, and still this locking symbol kept showing up. She was telling me that I needed to prove that the forks were hooked. The tires were torn to sh__t so that didn't help.

The cops have a propensity to take evidence like this, toss it and leave you with two bikes that have no tires, wheel rims, or much of anything to work with. The cycle the couple was driving was an old piece of junk essentially. The other cycle the third person was driving seemed like it was built to have a jet pack on it. Why anyone would ride one of those things, I don't know — to get the feeling of power I guess.

I had to research the motorcycles involved so contacted a motorcycle manufacturer and learned that it was more than probable that the two wheels of the motorcycles locked. This would be unlikely if they had been moving at close to the same speed. Then the wheels would bump and fly off, but these two bikes were traveling at very different speeds. The wheels can entangle even at a remarkably slow speed.
During the course of this investigation, I had to ask client M.K. about many things, and he wanted to know how I knew. Well, I certainly couldn't tell him the spirit prompted the specific questions. The D.A. would get a hold of that and say something like "Oh, so you're a psychic Mr. X" and case goes boom. In the end, the D.A. said, "You got me on this one," and the client was cleared of the charge of homicide by motor vehicle.

In my mind, it was through the insistence of this departed soul who wouldn't let go yet, that this case turned out as it did. Ghost, spirit, voice from out of nowhere? I don't know, but after this case was resolved, she didn't bother me any more.

The case of the ghostly lawyer

When you're doing Public Defender work, sometimes you have to wonder if you're starting to cover up for the client. If that's the case, then you definitely have to quit. I was nailing cases that blew my mind and cleared a number of clients. I had an interesting drug case about a young "drug dealer" who wasn't a drug dealer, but he was going to be put away for a long time because of the absurd and shortsighted truth-in-sentencing law bestowed upon us to contain the "worst of the worst" apparently. The young man was innocent. They wouldn't believe me, so I had to beat them to death with an affidavit.

Let me start from the beginning. A towing service was called to pick up a car that had hit a large deer. The boss of the service decided to take a second towing job and drop his employee off at the car that had been damaged by the deer, in order to drive the car back to the shop. The car was still drivable, but the car was tilted to one side, such that part of it crossed the centerline. The law decided to troll the area, and the car was pulled over. Of course, the young man's driver's license didn't match the vehicle identification of the car, and the law could not locate the owner at that point. They decided to search the car, and found four evenly cut quarters of marijuana.

Now the guy is under arrest, and had a prior conviction for pot smoking when he was 18 years old. So, this doesn't bid well for him. I don't condone pot smoking, but people do it, and that's the reality of it. They are hurting themselves. The county he was arrested in has a need for drug money, so they grab the case and run with it. The county used detectives from a neighboring county, and they kind of split the bust because they think it will lead to some fantastic drug operation somewhere.

I was called in on this case for the defendant. At the time I went to check it out, I got a stupid feeling of the *presence* of an older gentleman who was neatly dressed in a 1930's or 1940's suit. He had a distinguishable pin under his collar, resembling a nice piece of jewelry. The presence identified himself as an attorney and as a person of the family. Once again, I think I must be crazy, but this is where the case takes off. The ghostly lawyer says the only way to beat this is to find the real drug dealer before the authorities find him—and then I'm supposed to get an affidavit from him.

Now I hardly know all there is to know about the law, but as a Private Detective, I know what I need to know. But an affidavit? I had no idea what on earth that was going to do for this case. I went to the towing employee's place armed with a printer and a computer. The accused had no clue where the marijuana came from, and steadfastly denied that it was his. He sent me to see the owner of the car, and I talked with the car owner for about one and a half hours.

The dude's a compulsive type of guy, I end up spitting $20 of my hard-earned money out, and he tells me where the dealer is! As it turns out, the dealer thinks he's going to be busted, and therefore is leaving on an extended journey out of town. I do the interview, and Mr. Marijuana Dealer signs an affidavit. I notarize it. *Case Closed.* It even blew the judge away. I learned that the affidavit in this case is an extension of the judge's authority. The prosecutors for the two counties wanted my head on a platter at that point. They didn't think the judge would accept the affidavit.

The phantom lawyer wasn't a person, but I clearly perceived him, and he came with a message. My grandmother used to do the psychic medium thing at the table, and I thought it was a bunch of crap, but when you're dealing with situations like this, you have to question your beliefs. It has not been easy for me. I have seriously questioned my sanity, and not just as a passing thought. Talking about my past brings me to my memory of Gettysburg and the horrific Civil War battle. When I was a kid, I went to Gettysburg with my parents. We went past a building that was being remodeled, and in the window, I could see people stumped up—battle worn with arms and legs missing. I started screaming, yelling, and vomiting. At first, my parents thought I was pulling some kind of prank, and then they thought I was mentally ill, and then they thought I needed the Lord. After that, I was sent to a parochial high school.

The case of the distressed woman and a fussy Tylenol bottle

A woman from Milwaukee called me through a friend of hers to check the strange things happening in the lady's apartment. It was just an ordinary apartment building with nothing wrong, but it had a resonance to it. Immediately, I took note of the layout of the place, and the arrangement of the furniture. On a small table next to a rocking chair, she had configured some things, which included a glass of soda and a Tylenol bottle. She noted that every time she'd put the Tylenol bottle away, she'd hear a slam of the medicine cabinet door and the bottle would appear once again on the table. Normally, I'd question this, but it happened while I was there. We didn't see the Tylenol bottle move. It was when we'd look away and then look back at the table, that the bottle would just be there. This was repeated several times. It was as if she was denying somebody the Tylenol bottle.

My theory is that the configuration of the room had somehow brought back someone's memory of the room the way it had been at a previous point in time. The woman also complained that the TV would turn on when the show *Jeopardy* was scheduled to air. I don't know how true this is, because I wasn't there to witness it. I believe the whole thing had to do with resonance. If you are a person who is sensitive, almost like a radio receiver, you have these things happen to you. Psychic people have trauma in their lives that allow them to open to this. It's almost a prerequisite. I know the Tylenol lady had trauma in her life.

I think the ghosts are humans once living, but now without a body. Space and time become factors. It was said to me that *time* here, might be *space* in another dimension or state. If you travel from one room to the next, it will be a different time and a different memory, but it doesn't go away. So, if you are replicating something that was in a departed person's memory, that entity will be right there with you. That's why the Tylenol bottle is so frustrating. It turns out that a tenant had terrible arthritis, and this was in the days before the Advil experience. He always had his Tylenol bottle and a glass of water in the same area that she usually had a glass of soda and a Tylenol bottle. The configuration and the layout of the room evidently replicated the way his life was, so I surmise, he just assumed he was at home.

In real lifetime, he probably argued with his wife about the Tylenol bottle being part of the living room décor. Was this a ghost? Was this a poltergeist phenomenon? I don't know. We rearranged the room to take it out of the familiar configuration, and the problem stopped. This type of phenomenon happen all the time. How many times have you had weird little things disappear, and days later the item is back at the spot where you left it before?

The case of a boy and a river

We asked Mr. X, if someone asks you to check out a house, do you do it? What do you tell them?

Yes, I will usually go into a house. I tell them what I see or what I am experiencing. But if something is grotesque or disgusting, and would likely affect them negatively, it serves no purpose to tell them everything. That's the problem with this. Unscrupulous people will say you have an evil monster in here, and something awful has happened, and I will get rid of it for 250 bucks. It doesn't work that way. A woman called me up to say she was having problems with her son. Sometime before that, I had read her palm, so she was a little familiar with me. "My son is yelling and screaming and speaking in strange languages and I don't know what to do; I don't know what's wrong!" She wanted me to promise that I would not discuss this in detail [like in *Dragnet*: names are changed to protect the innocent] so I won't go further except to say the boy was affected by his surroundings.

I asked if there was a river near by, and was his bed perpendicular to the river. Indeed, there was a river within about 250 feet of the house, and yes indeed, his bed was perpendicular to it. I asked her to change the direction of the bed so that it was parallel to the water flow. She did this, and the craziness ceased. For whatever reason, this perpendicular configuration was driving him nuts. Maybe for most people, the position of the bed would be inconsequential. I don't have an explanation for why changing his surroundings took care of the problem. All I can say is that the brain is an electromagnetic device so it has to have "rules." There's no magic in this. It's more complex than the way I am presenting it, of course. But when our brain thinks, we increase and decrease the amount of electricity that we use, and we use this to communicate with other parts of the brain. I believe that when a person dies, this process does not go away, just the physical body does.

The case of the perturbed mother ghost

A ghost usually has no idea it's bothering you. A ghost is reliving life. But when you make things resonate with the way the person had things, the person may react by reappearing and interacting with you. This can be disturbing and just plain annoying.

A woman, Ms. B, was scheduled to be on a TV show that I was filming, but she was in the middle of remodeling her recently deceased mother's house, so was apprehensive about participating in the show. The woman didn't know this, but the deceased mother started to bother *me* way before this remodeling project began. Mother was having a fit. She did not like what they were doing with the kitchen. I think the woman was actually a jerk when she was amongst the living, and she was certainly carrying her bad attitude into death.

Again, I thought I was losing my mind. The moment

time. A family of a mother, father and child said they had been killed in a fire shortly after the turn of the century. The family had been living in an apartment that was upstairs and behind the place. Indeed, a fire had occurred in the building as they claimed. Scott had uncovered burnt timbers when he was renovating along with evidence of the date of the fire.

An elderly black man came through on the tape, as did a black woman who claimed to have been a hard working cook. A gentleman calling himself "grandpa" was on the tape. He may have been the man who operated the Western Auto in the same location in the fifties.

The building next door was apparently a hotel. People would gather around an old tree that was once there. This building had been used for 125 years for many different kinds of shops. The collective memories are stored around the site supposedly, but not forever, as Scott and others were told later. Kathleen said the spirits indicated that they liked what I had done to the place, but didn't like the color of the walls. They said that some of them would be moving on and "we're glad you're back." Scott had not thought about an existence in a past life, if that's what the spirits were referring to that day.

Kathleen pointed out that the walk-in cooler seemed to be a vortex of energy, like a cosmic whirlpool. She talked about one place in the kitchen where she felt like something was descending. As it turns out, a stairway leading to the basement was once in that location. Scott had taken it out when he remodeled the building. It was now covered with two inches of plywood and a layer of linoleum. Near the front of the restaurant, Kathleen pointed to an area in the floor and made a circular motion with her hand. She said that she was getting the sense of something "round" here. "We knew of nothing, and she was pointing to a crawl space with the dirt barely a foot below the floor. I had no idea what she was talking about."

Scott said that after he closed the restaurant, his mother, Frances, replaced it with an antique store, and operated it for many years. However, about three years after taking over the building, a major plumbing problem developed under the building, and the main pipes underneath the shop had to be replaced. The plumber doing the work reported that he nearly fell into an old well or cistern that was about four feet in diameter and fifteen feet deep. This was exactly the spot where Kathleen had indicated there was "something round" in this area a few years earlier.

Scott's comments

Scott said that he had a long time to reflect on the revelations of the day Kathleen entered his restaurant. As a result, he says, "Reincarnation, ghosts, psychic phenomenon have a meaning to me now. I realized I had an instant attraction to Madison, Georgia from the first time I saw the place. It is definitely my home. When I drive to work in the morning and it's foggy, I sometimes get little glimpses, freeze frames, of trees standing alone in a pasture. For a split second, I see the trees in the present and the past. I remember the time, and then it's gone. When people talk about small town individuals, they often label them as the 'been here' folks and the 'come here' folks. I propose we add a new category of the 'back here' folks."

In a recent interview with us, Kathleen said:

I remember the Horse and Hound Café as a constant parade of "people" going through the room. The cooler was like a portal — a hole in time — a passageway between now and times past. Perhaps this would account for some of the forgetfulness people had while in the cooler. As far as the spirits not liking the color of the walls, I don't think they appreciate "their" territory being altered. They can be fussy, and act out in ways such as creating noises, banging, footsteps, and so on. That sort of thing really does get our attention! The spirits in this case seemed pleased to have "my ear" to hear them. It's as if they had been waiting a long time to be heard.

And as far as the plumbing problem in the antique store, I clearly recall making the circles with my arms, and saying that there was something round in this area. And I remember Scott firmly saying, "No, there is nothing under that floor but dirt!"

I held my ground and politely informed him, "Yes there is!" At that point, I let it go, but I'm so glad the plumber did not fall into the old well. I believe that one or more of the unseen residents intervened on his behalf — lucky for him.

For the record

Kathleen would like to set things straight and inform us that she was never on a bowling league, and has not been a smoker for several years now. She does admit to the "screaming Wis-can-sen" accent however, and thinks Scott is a "nice, personable, young man."

Kathleen's active practice as a psychic, medium, and spiritual consultant began in 1979. Over the past 26 years, she interviewed numerous times for print media, and appeared on local television and radio. She is also featured in the book Famous Wisconsin Mystics *(by H.H. Levy, Badger Books, 2003). Her practice is in Middleton, Wisconsin (phone: 608-836-1935) (E-mail: ksmystic@mailstation.com).*

Personal Accounts Gathered by Roving Writer Brian Borton

Brian goes to the Bar Next Door

The energetic roving collector of ghost stories, Brian Borton, took the show on the road, and traveled to several ghostly destinations. He started out at a place formerly known as the Wonder Bar, now The Bar Next Door in Madison, Wisconsin—a place he was strangely attracted to and felt he was being "watched" while conducting the interviews. He's not a shy guy, so he journeyed on despite the unseen audience.

What's the history behind the mystery?

The first interview comes from former staff member at the Bar Next Door, Cory Guessler. He conducted a bit of research and found out that it was built in 1929 by Roger "The Terrible" Touhey and his brother George. The infamous Roger was a brewer in Chicago whose specialty was bootleg beer. Gangster Al Capone made a move to capture the bootleg industry, and "kicked out" Roger, essentially. Roger set up roadhouses in Eau Claire, Madison, and Sauk Prairie. This was basically a front for the Irish mob. Roger the Terrible was the leader of Chicago's Irish gang based in Des Plaines, Illinois. The little place he set up in Madison just happened to be a convenient wayside stop for illegal alcohol to stretch its tentacles and invade further north.

Cory tells the story: The roadhouse was known as the Wonder Bar until the late 1980's. In the 1990's it became the MOB Road House, so named by owner Mike O'Brien (thus the M-O-B). In 1997, it was taken over by Pete Beever, and then it became The Bar Next Door. Never fear however, the walls are bulletproof and quarter-inch steel. And for the gang's quick get-away during Prohibition, the building is equipped with its own tunnel from the northeast corner of the building out to Lake Monona. The tunnel was sealed off in the 1960s by the city of Madison for safety reasons.

The building, with its turret-style roof, has nook and cranny hiding places to stash booze, and discrete compartments under the windowsills, not coincidentally just the right size to hold a submachine gun. The back had big garage doors where trucks could pull in and drop off a delivery of the contraband. Touhey supposedly lived a mile south-southwest on Lacey Road in a place that was only visible in the wintertime. He could see to the far reaches of Madison across the farm fields, and was on the lookout for "Feds" just in case he'd have to "move a few things."

I remember in the summer of 1998 a tall blonde girl came into the bar—you know kind of Amazon-type. She brought a friend who was a psychic. The psychic believed a big husky guy frequented the poolroom area in times past where he guarded the backdoor. She believed that a child played downstairs, and another guy was tied up in the downstairs.

The upstairs area of the establishment was a burlesque house, and the stairs going upstairs, used to be outside. The girls living next door used the side entrance that originally led to the upstairs. Today the upstairs is a manager's office, a liquor cabinet, two bathrooms and a second poolroom.

What haunting experiences have you had in this place?

I'd go to the basement to bring up some ice, get French

fires, or change kegs. The first couple of times I thought it was cool, intriguing—old building, you know. I'm a "throw back" who probably should have been born in the 1930's. After a time, I began to get a real weird feeling. I was uneasy. That's the best way to describe it, because I didn't feel there was anything evil or ominous present. It was eerie and creepy.

I would catch things out of the corner of my eye. I don't know if it was just my imagination or not. When I'd be down by the ice machine, it was slightly warm because the motor was running, but every now and then I'd hit cold spots, and breezes would brush past my ears. As I mentioned, the psychic said there had been a guy tied up by the ice machine, and also a little girl played in the basement. The psychic told me to address myself when I was down there, and to let them know I'm here. Ever since I've done this, I've never felt creepy—no cold sensations or breezes.

Other odd things have happened. We had neon signs upstairs by the windows. My routine was to start on the east end, turn the last light off and head downstairs. One of the first times that I was closing the place, I'd turn off the last neon light and the first one goes on! So, I walk over and turn that one off, and the last one goes on. Now, I'm sure the place is haunted. I had to say, "It is 3:30 A.M., I'm tired, it's Friday night, I'm trying to close the place down, and I just want to go home and go to bed. Please leave me alone." The annoying playful activity stopped, and I was able to turn off the lights without this leapfrog game continuing.

I've heard stories from other people, but another actual experience that I personally had, occurred one night in the late fall. We seem to have paranormal activity around here every four to six months. Activity spikes for a few weeks, and then there is nothing. Anyway, I remember late October or early November, and Monday night football was on TV. Around 11:00 at night, a woman was sitting at the bar reading a book. I left her alone, but waited on her of course. She went to the restroom, came back and ordered a glass of wine.

We started to visit a little, and she ordered another glass of wine. By now, it's 11:30. All of a sudden, a light flashed between us. I attributed it to some kind of power surge or a wiring thing, until the woman said, "Did you just see something fly between us?" Now I get the goose bumps. That just creeped me out! I told her that I did see…something. I never would have thought about it, had she not said anything. And of course, wouldn't you know it; I'm closing the bar that night—alone. Yup, home alone. I don't know if I was talking this up in my imagination, or what, but I could have sworn somebody walked by the dart machine. I had all the lights off except the bar lights. I just caught a glimpse out of the corner of my eye.

Another incident happened during one of those spike-in-activity periods. I was working at the bar, and suddenly I heard this loud crash coming from upstairs. Nobody was up there at the time, so I went running to see what had happened. The picture of Al Capone that was hanging on the wall, decided to take flight I guess, and was lying halfway across the room. Well, that picture had a makeshift frame to begin with, but you'd think that if it were going to fall, it would just crash straight down, not several feet across the room. The frame was in pieces. I tend to think that the ghost did not exactly appreciate a picture of Al Capone hanging in this neck of the woods.

I tell myself, Cory, it's always the lights with you…

Sometimes I'd come into work and forget to turn a few of the lights on …it's always the lights with me…or the day person would turn them on ahead of me. One day Shawn and Kristin were downstairs doing inventory, and I was opening up the place. The lights were off, and I made absolutely sure that the lights were turned on in the barroom. Then I went upstairs to turn on those lights, and all the lights in the whole place were on—upstairs, hallway, bathroom, above the pool table—every possible light is on! I thought to myself, okay, cool, nice that my co-workers helped me out. I went downstairs to thank the two workers for turning the lights on for me, and they said that they hadn't touched them. Maybe they were pulling my leg; I don't really know, but they seemed dead serious and even a little frightened—just had an unsettling feeling.

The guy with the crazy blonde hair...

This character with crazy-looking blonde hair came into the bar one Monday night and said, "Has anything weird happened here?" He was in town on business, and was probably thirty-ish. I said, something like, "What...like girls jumping on the bar or something?" I didn't know what he was getting at. Then he said, "No, I mean *paranormal*." I said that I had a couple of stories. One of them was the story about Bubba, one of the first bartenders here. Bubba wanted to make sure nobody was upstairs at closing time; didn't want anybody hiding out after hours. At that time, there was really nothing up there except an office. Bubba saw a man on the stairs wearing a fedora and trench coat, and said, "Hey buddy, we're closing here." The bartender continued up the stairs, but turned around to make sure Mr. Fedora-trench coat was leaving. To his total amazement, nobody was in sight.

Another bartender, Matt, told the same story a week earlier, and neither bartender realized that each of them had had the same experience. Matt had done the same thing—he informed a man with a fedora hat who was on the stairway that the place was closing for the night. "Skeptic" is Matt's middle name for as long as I've known him. The man with the wild blonde hair listened without commenting. I continued talking, no surprise there. On a Friday or Saturday night when the bartenders were back in the pool table room near closing, no other lights were on in the building except for in that poolroom. The bartenders would be smoking and joking, and having a couple of beers after a long night bartending.

Matt would turn around and there'd be a man at the end of the bar watching him. The guy had on a trench coat and a fedora hat. So, I told Wild Hair Blonde guy this story.

Now Kristin, another bartender, told bartender Rick that she had a customer come in the week before the picture flew off the wall. The customer's name was Alex. The customer said, "Kristin, I'm going to ask you a weird question. Do you have ghosts here? I think I heard it was haunted, and I think I actually just saw one." Customer Alex was going upstairs to the bathroom by the office, and Mr. Trench Coat-Fedora appeared in the hallway. Alex said, "Hi, how are you doing?" The customer did not know these stories about the guy in the hat and trench coat prior to this.

So now, I tell Blonde Guy this...

...and silent Blonde Guy speaks up to tell me that when he was young he had a near-death experience. Because of this, he has the ability to see and talk to ghosts, and interact. I'm thinking...ya, right, but I suppose he could have some kind of paranormal or para-psychoses type of ability to interact with the spirit world. I don't know if that's impossible or not. Blonde Guy said that three months prior to talking with me, he talked to bartender Pete, and asked him the same thing. Then Blonde Guy told me a story. On that particular night that he had been talking with Pete, the bar was particularly noisy, and people were throwing dice. So Blonde Guy decided to go back to his room at the Sheraton Hotel. He said, "I sat in the car, and looked over at the passenger side, and there's this guy in a trench coat and hat sitting in the car. "Hey buddy, you can't go with me," I said. "Oh ya, by the way," said Blonde Guy, "they follow you around."

Cory hears creaky noises...

I think I might have been followed home once too. I was alone at my place and heard creaky noises that I had not heard before. You know how you get used to the little noises here and there. Maybe it was my mind playing tricks on me because Blonde Guy said they could follow you home. I can't pinpoint any sounds in particular.

But getting back to Blonde Guy, after telling me the story he said, "I'm going to give you something, but you have to promise me that you won't spend it." He gave me a dollar bill, and on it was written the words, "keep me; don't spend." I have kept this in my wallet ever since that night. Before that, I had not actually experienced anything that I would consider paranormal. I had just heard stories. Blonde Guy said, "But now this [dollar bill] is touched by one of us; you'll start to experience things." About a week later, that's when the lights started going crazy. With me, it's always with the lights, you know.

Big Eric enters...

One night I had a guy named Eric come into the bar. He and his buddies look like punk rockers—big guys, a rough-looking bunch. They live on east Gilson and on the other side of Olin Avenue from where I lived—same block. For some reason, the topic of ghosts came up, and I told them the three stories about the hat and trench coat guy; the same stories I told you. Eric said, "Shut up; you're pulling my leg, nah...shut up." Then Eric got dead serious. "You are pulling my leg, aren't you? Cory, that guy was at my house. He shows up with a black cat that wanders around the house. None of us owns pets. We see him now and then."

Cory continues. I think the trench coat guy either lived at this residence, or he might have been part of the mob that just watched the roadhouse. Maybe he was somebody like me who worked here, and is keeping an eye on the place. I've never seen a full body apparition of Mr. Trench Coat and I don't know if I'd want to see one. It would be great to find out what his name was, and what his relationship to the bar was. Did he just love this place? What happened?

Was he buried in the chimney?

I don't know if Mr. Trench Coat was buried in the chimney or not. I don't know much about that, but there is a secret chamber in the fireplace. My friend Tony has a grandfather who knew people in the Irish mob, but he won't talk to anybody. If anybody wants to talk to him about the old days, grandpa always goes through Tony. I guess there is a secret lever on the fireplace that moves the front of the fireplace out. Tony almost had grandpa convinced to talk about it, but he's pretty closed-mouthed. We can tell that the fireplace is attached to the wall—solid, but if you feel underneath, you can feel the metal and different levers. When we put the carpeting down, we saw wear marks on the floor.

Speculation says there might be a stash of something back there, but nobody around here knows. Other stories that have surrounded the place say that the fireplace crypt holds the bones of a Touhey brother killed in a shootout. Another tale says that a person who crossed the Touhey brothers met his demise, and was buried behind the fireplace. There are two fireplaces upstairs. Now, I don't know what's going on with that old fireplace, but one night it was very late…

Pete Beever takes the floor…
Okay Pete, so what's your story?

I was sleeping in front of the gas fireplace right after I closed the place up one night. It had been a long twelve-hour day, and periodically, I just stay here. All of a sudden, I'm startled and wake up abruptly. Believe me I was wide-awake. I heard something in the back, and then I found myself starring at the fireplace. Strangely, the gas fireplace had gone out completely. I can't explain it, and it's never happened before. This happened just at the time I had to leave to pick up my daughter. It was a very odd occurrence.

I had heard that when Jessica was tending bar here she felt like something was holding her hair up. She looked in the mirror and saw that her hair was actually standing out as if someone were holding it up. Whether this was embellished or not, I don't know, but Jessica says she will never be in the building alone again. Another story comes from Mike Harms, one of the bar managers. He said that he had all of these cigar boxes behind the bar as decoration. One by one, they started flipping over. Again, that's not first had information that I have. We had a medium go downstairs once and she said she could see men in black slacks and white shirts. Who knows what that is, or what that means!

How about those cold spots?

Cold spots? Ya, you know it's an old building, and it's hard to say how that works, but I've noticed it can be as hot as hell in there, and when you close down it gets unusually cold—more than you'd expect a place to cool down. I've heard about the woman ghost, but I've never seen her. I hadn't heard about the little girl playing downstairs.

Do you believe in ghosts?

Yes, there's no doubt about it after working here at the Bar Next Door. But it depends on what the description of a ghost is. We've had a couple of dogs in here a few times, but they pretty much sat in the corner. Why do I believe in ghosts? Maybe some people believe in the phenomenon to be able to accept certain situations. People look for reasons when things happen, but the answers don't come in an easy way.

What do you know about the history of the Bar Next Door?

It was built in 1921 by the Touhey family who ran the northwest side of Chicago. They controlled a lot of unions, and beer distributorships during prohibition. They originally started in the oil business, but there was an oil shortage at the time and the trucks sat empty. So, instead of filling them with oil, they filled them with beer. At the time, they supplied Al Capone with beer, but he began taking over the business. The Touhey's then built roadhouses in the Midwest, and one of the places was the Wonder Bar, now known as the Bar Next Door. The walls are bullet proof, and there are turrets at each corner. Five FBI files exist on the Touhey family. Roger Touhey was the leader of the gang and wrote a book titled *The Stolen Years.* The Wonder Bar is mentioned in the book.

Kristen Olshanski, bar manager, adds to the mystery…

The brother and sister ran the restaurant. It kind of looks like a house, but it was designed to be a restaurant. The upstairs had three bedrooms and a bathroom, and I'm told that gangsters running up north used this as a stopping place or hideout. Women next door entertained the men. What happened here stayed here, and you had to know somebody to stay here. Now the tunnel has been closed off because the city said it might collapse. It was used as an escape that runs underneath the basement stairs out towards the lake.

What impresses you about the place as far as haunting?

When it was remodeled there was a fireplace added. It sounds strange because there's already one fireplace in the room. But the original fireplace was designed not to work. It's just for show and there's no flue. The story is that there's somebody in our fireplace. When we remodeled up here, the plan was to take that old fireplace out, and then the plan was ditched at the last minute. We decided that if somebody were in there, we didn't want to disrupt that.

I get a lot of eclectic types up here. They meditate to the beat of an Indian drum, and they say that they see all kinds of spirits up here. Other people who are not psychic come in here and describe a man and a woman. Whether they've heard stories or not, or know anything about them, they describe the same people. Many people who come up here say there's negative energy coming from the old fireplace.

We had the Southern Wisconsin Paranormal Research Group come in here, and their equipment was going off from upstairs to downstairs — from the fireplace area down through the basement. Someone says the area serves as an antenna. We have been told that this always must be a bar or a bar-restaurant because no other business would succeed in this building. The haunting would get worse. I like to say we get along with the ghosts and they are happy here. You get the feeling that you're never alone and that you're always being observed.

One ring phone call at 3 A.M.
Have you had any personal experiences here?

I am here alone a lot. The first night I closed by myself, I felt a poking in the middle of my back. It's not as if they were touching me, but it was a poking sensation. I thought that maybe it was a muscle spasm or something. I finally said, "If you're here, that's great, but I'm not ready to meet you. You can't hang out here." I'm not ready to see them; that's my biggest thing. I get the feeling they don't like me, but I'm not afraid.

Plenty of people have worked here, have been frightened by something, and have never come back!

When you go upstairs, you feel that someone is right on your heels, and the hair on the back of your neck stands up. Usually this happens when you're coming up from the basement. What really freaks me out is that the phone rings on many nights at 3 A.M. I'd say this happens twice a week, and this continues until the place is closed up. If you catch the phone immediately and try to answer it, you get a dial tone. It's as if the phone is calling itself and then hanging up after one ring. It seems like we don't have any occurrences for months, and then we get a cluster.

Beeping noises, glasses clinking...

Around Halloween, weird customers visit this place. Kimberly and I were working here one night around that time. We were closing and had loud music playing, but then over the music, we heard a loud high-pitch beeping. We thought that maybe it was a lost cell phone with a message coming in or something. So I got on my hands and knees to look for the cell phone. Maybe it's just the song. No, I've heard this song before. About ten minutes later, we heard glasses clinking around the pool table, and we thought that maybe it was the place next door just dumping out bottles. But I checked it out, and that wasn't it either. So now, we have a ghost trying to send a text message on cell phone, and another one setting the table for us!

Then the phone started ringing, and we heard what sounded like furniture shifting around, as if somebody was doing something really productive in the back hallway. We thought maybe we should check it out, but Kimberly said, "No, nobody is in here. We're just going to let it be." Kimberly doesn't believe in any of this stuff. When things happen, she just says, "That was weird, and I don't want to talk about it." We thought, well, whoever or whatever this is, just stay here, and then we left. Despite her not believing in ghosts, Kimberly has seen bottles literally jump off the shelf and break far from where they should have logically fallen.

Do you remember a picture falling off the wall? How about the delivery guy?

It was a Packer Sunday and Pete had left for the day. We heard a big thud, like a bar stool falling over. Cory said, "Oh, that was Pete." But Pete had already left, so we went upstairs and there's the picture of Al Capone lying face up at least four feet from the wall. We've always said that Roger is slapping us in the face for calling it Capone's Bar Next Door instead of Touhey's. I think Capone ultimately killed Touhey—bad karma here or something.

I have a beer delivery guy who is terrified of this place. Something happens to him every time. He's been delivering beer here for years — big tough guy. When he's here in the basement, he sees a flash of somebody, the lights go out, or he finds himself locked in and can't get out. Getting locked in is strange, since the building locks from the inside. He was here fixing the keg line two months ago, and he kept running up and down the basement stairs checking on the keg line. His tools kept being moved. I said, "Ray, do you have this fixed yet? This is ridiculous."

Ray said that every time he came up to the bar to see if the line was running, he'd end up running back down to the basement to find that the line had been shut off. A switch controls opening up the lines from the basement. Ray doesn't understand it, and he doesn't like it, but it keeps happening anyhow. It's annoying to him.

Do you believe the place is haunted?

Yes. I don't want to judge it, but there have been times when I've felt uncomfortable enough to think that maybe I shouldn't be working here. But it's weird. You can't really put on a resume that you left a job because of the ghosts. "Charlie" is what I call the well-dressed, portly guy in the trench coat with matching fedora. Sometimes the coat is described as a jacket. The woman in the dress has been seen back by the hallway. She's described with brownish-red hair and a white dress I think.

The last thing I want to do is run into a ghost at 3 A.M. I didn't want the research people to come here, because in the past when people have come to explore, the activity has gotten worse. I said to the Southern Wisconsin Paranormal Research Group that if things were going to get worse, I didn't want them here. Jennifer, from the group, said that actually thing usually improve. When I opened the place to let them set up, all the chairs were on the table. How weird is that! I was the only one in here between the time I left and the time that they arrived.

Energy on vacation and place runs amok...

The research group didn't record many readings, except for a significant reading that shot through the whole building from top to bottom. To me, in general, it was as if the energy was hiding out when they were here. I came into work on Monday and Tuesday, and there was just no energy in the place, as if it had all left on vacation. You know how your home has certain vibes, well, so does this place. I didn't feel like I was being watched, like I usually feel, and the atmosphere was eerily calm. For those two days, I had the worst customers.

We are so lucky—no fights, no drugs, and so on. I had people in here who were just loony. My guess is they should have been on medications and they were not. Other people gave me such a hard time. I thought to myself, if this is a permanent change, and these are the kind of customers we're getting, then I can't work here. I can't deal with these people on a daily basis and have my normal customers—two days of hell and miserable customers.

On Wednesday, I was closing up at 3A.M. and the phone rang. I had a friend here at the time, and he looked at me and said, "That was weird." I didn't say anything and I didn't bother to pick up the phone because I knew it would be just one ring. I thought to myself, good they're back! I haven't had problems with customers since then. I always thought that Pete was not telling me everything when I started to work here. Then there was the fireplace incident where the gas fireplace shut off by itself. In all of my days here, that fireplace has never gone off. You have to turn a knob to shut it down.

Mickey's Tavern

The place has an interesting history, I'm told.

Bob Hemauer of Mickey's tells us that Mickey's was built
in 1902 by Henry Niebuhr for $5000. It's probably the oldest
continuously operated bar in Madison, and it definitely has
its own personality that covers every era. Henry ran the bar
until 1920 and then Mickey took it over with his brother.
It ran through Prohibition, and was a boarding house along
with a tavern when it first opened. The upper rooms were for
boarders and the owner's apartment was in the back. When
the circus hit Madison, a lot of those folks would stay here.

In 1912, the traveling Buffalo Bill's Wild West Show
came to town. A member of the show was shot over at the
bar where Commonwealth now stands. He died on the front
steps entry of Mickey's. The carnies hauled the body away,
and the death was never reported. This part of town was a
rough and tumble working area. There were a lot of factories
on East Washington Avenue. In the 1930's, Mickey and his
brother ran a barbershop, a grocery store, and a soda fountain
where they were bootlegging liquor.

Mickey's brother had a bad habit of drinking behind the
bar when he was working. A federal agent came to the bar,
and the brother offered him a drink. The feds came back later
and asked where the booze was hidden. The way the stairs was
set up, all the booze was kept in the wall. The feds couldn't
find it, so they threatened to bust the place up. Instead, the
bar was busted for bootlegging. The area around here used
to be marshland, and much of the liquor was stashed in the
marshy area by the railroad tracks.

Mickey's brother died of tuberculosis in the 1940's and
Mickey sold the bar to his son and daughter-in-law in the mid
1970's. Mickey lived upstairs where I live now. He said that
if he ever left this building he would die. When he went to a
nursing home at age 96, he died within the month. He had a
lot of health problems at that point. Mickey's wife, Pearl, used

to sit at the end of the bar, and carve things with a straw. The bar has been in the Niebuhr family for a hundred years.

What's been going on in regards to paranormal activity?

Unexplainable experiences include people feeling a cold rush of air, hearing footsteps, and seeing figures. One of the bartenders walking down the basement stairs saw a woman to the left out of the corner of her eye. The bartender turned, and the woman was gone. The former manager, named Brian, lived upstairs in the apartment. He saw an apparition of a man at the top of the stairs clutching his chest. Another bartender and his girlfriend found that two plants had been taken out of their pots and put in the sink. Random weirdness takes place, but I've made peace. I think the ghost is Mickey. He would resent this new Willy Street.

In my apartment upstairs, I have an old poster of Mao's Cultural Revolution in China. It's a cool poster—Mao smoking a cigarette, and so on. I had this poster on a 75-pound picture hook hanger. It was firmly placed on that hanger. One day I found that the poster had fallen off the wall and was impossibly in the middle of the room. The picture hanger was still in the wall—now that is weird. Glass shattered and scattered everywhere. All of the other pictures remained on the wall.

Another thing that happened was that I bought a glass top bar for up in the apartment. I put it together, and the glass cracked down the center. I know there were no temperature fluctuations, and I had a level on it, so I know the glass was not bowed. I don't have an explanation, other than the ghost just makes a lot of nuisance. Nothing ever happens in the main bar, just every place else. Machines randomly turn on, items become misplaced, and every once in a while a figure will appear. Dogs bark at things, but it's hard to tell if they're barking at anything abnormal or not.

Have you ever had the place investigated?

No. Nobody feels threatened. Sometimes the entities might seem aggressive, but it doesn't affect anybody's quality of life here. I believe there are things here that are paranormal, but I don't want to disturb whatever it is, as long as they don't bother me. A handful of bartenders have heard footsteps in the back, but I try to write it off as something else, so let my rational mind take over. We've experienced no odd scents or odors. Lights definitely do go on and off again in the basement. Part of me thinks it is an old electrical system, but we've rewired and it still happens. Sometimes a light will be on, but the switch will be off.

Do you believe in ghosts?

I'm really skeptical about the unexplainable. I don't believe in God either, but when you consider the sum total of all that goes on here, well...maybe something is up. I think that when you die, you're just dead, but there are too many things here to discount it. Before I started working here, I actively made fun of people who believed in ghosts—crazy, stupid people. I tried to explain the stuff. The light is on because...well, no, the switch turns them *all* on or *all* off, so *one* light on is impossible. I tried to rationalize, but the picture thing totally freaked me out. Mickey was not fond of communists, so the Mao poster might have been too much to tolerate. Generally, things happen upstairs more so than downstairs. There were transients who came in and out of here, and in the early part of the century, this was not good for the neighborhood.

A patron of Mickey's has a word...

Are you a believer in ghosts or the supernatural? Why is there a need to believe?

I'm not a disbeliever. I think unexplainable things happen sometimes, and the easiest thing to attribute the unexplainable to is a ghost. People seem to have a need to know, or to believe that people who have passed away are still around and can communicate in some way.

Anything happen to you here at Mickey's?

I was sitting at the end of the bar here once, and nobody was within four feet of me at least. No one was walking behind me, but suddenly I heard a gruff older man's voice. I thought that had to be impossible. It sounded like it was six inches away and was talking in my ear. The oldest person in this place was probably about 30. Really, it did not sound like a younger man at all. This voice was of somebody who was sixty or seventy. I finished the drink and went home.

Jingles Coliseum Bar

Karen Krueger gave us the story behind Jingles. The ghost is named Marlene, and she died of a stroke or an aneurysm in the restaurant. I've worked here three years, and I knew I had to say hello to her when I unlocked the building. She never hurt anybody that I know of. She likes to rearrange things. I'd be restocking, and one of the bottles that I brought up from storage would disappear. After I'd go down to get another one to replace the missing bottle, it would show up again.

Marlene also likes to turn the lights on. I'd be locking up for the night, have all the lights turned off, and going out to my car, and then I'd see that the lights were on again! Once we heard a loud crash in the kitchen. You'd think there would be plates scattered all over, because that's what it sounded like. We went to the kitchen, and it looked like nothing had happened. We never figured it out.

I personally have not seen any apparitions. I open and close the place. There's more activity at night when I'm getting ready to close. We had swinging doors that were off the kitchen and a liquor room. Another person, Dave, was here alone and all four doors began swinging simultaneously. He was so frightened that he never returned to the building unless someone was with him.

Something rather bizarre happened with one of those claw machines. It's a machine where you deposit the money, and then move the arm to pick up the prize. One night the arm came out, opened and closed, and it never dropped down to pick up an object. Another employee was with me and saw this too. We called a person from the vending machine company that owned the machine, and he came out to check on it. He found nothing wrong with the machine. It was in proper working order. Not five minutes after the vending machine man left, the claw arm moved again. It was not moving on its own, but I don't know what was moving it.

Are you a believer in ghosts?

I don't really believe in things unless I see them for myself. Therefore, I don't really believe in ghosts either, but some pretty strange things have happened, so my lean is to consider what's happened at this place. One night two waitresses and I were at the bar with a friend. I was closing the register. We have those large industrial fans here that create a windblast, and one just kicked on by itself. I didn't think much of it—thought maybe there was a short in the wire or something. My friend went around the corner to unplug it, and said, "Uhmmm…it's not plugged in." It was going full blast for a time.

The chairs moved once, but I wasn't here to witness that. They are plastic chairs that cannot be stacked more than five high. For some reason, stacking them higher causes them to tip. A group of people was here to set up for a banquet, and the chairs were stacked four high at the time. The group went to the barroom as they planned how they wanted to set up this room. When they returned to the banquet room, the chairs were stacked to the ceiling.

We had to tip over about 250 chairs, and then pull them apart to move them back into place. Most of the activity is in the barroom, backrooms, and banquet room. People are obliged to say hello to ghost Marlene. When I'm busy, I don't know if something is missing, but when it's quiet, I notice things out of place.

My other experience with haunting is when I lived on Johnson Street in Madison. Supposedly, a little boy in white makes his appearance once in a while. The cat noticed things and meowed, and the cat would stare at the ceiling and meow at it. The "ghost" seemed to be able to move the cats. I would keep the cats in my room at night. There was no way they could get out of my room except through the doorway, which I kept closed. My roommate was in another room, and would often find the cat sitting on his bed. We looked in the closet to see if the cat could get out that way, but there was no way. We never figured this mystery out.

Ominous Ontario Street
Madison

I rented the four-bedroom house that was built in 1956 on Ontario Street. Three instances have me thinking something really could be out there that is unexplainable to us. I was with my daughter when she was about one and a half. We were sitting in the living room. A hallway connected the kitchen to the living room. I noticed that she was looking at the kitchen. We were by ourselves in the house, and for some reason she headed towards the kitchen, but I could still keep an eye on her. Suddenly I heard a crash. My daughter was just wide-eyed at that point, and her body tensed up. It was as if a plate had crashed, but I could see her, so I knew that nothing had been broken. She was shaking by this time, and just crying and crying.

Now I'm thinking there's something in this house! I went to the kitchen, and everything was in place. Both doors to the kitchen were locked, and there's no way anybody could get into the house. I was just totally freaked out. I was tell-

The Bar Next Door in Madison is reportedly haunted by a few ghosts, the most notorious being the man in the trench coat. (Photo by Brian Borton)

ing this to the landlord at the time my roommate was here. Then I asked the landlord if the place was haunted. He said, no, and he had lived here for three years himself. Okay, my roommate is now almost going crazy. His eyes widened and he firmly said to me, "Don't even say that!" The week before he thought he saw somebody walk into the laundry room out of the corner of his eye, while he was cleaning his room, which is directly across from the laundry room. He thought someone was in the house, so he grabbed his baseball bat. He went to the laundry room and nobody was there.

Three weeks after all this, I was upstairs sleeping. I had not been drinking. I was just upstairs watching a movie and I feel asleep. I woke up with a startle, and I looked around my room. In my closet, I saw the silhouette of somebody who is a little stockier than I am. His arms were at his side, he was blonde, and faceless. It was a dark silhouette, but you could tell the hair was blonde. I lied down again and rubbed my eyes, and then tilted my head up again to see this thing in my closet again. Am I dreaming again, or what? I look again and it's gone. So I go over to the closet and I see a "baby" on the floor. I rub my eyes again, and look at the baby who appears to be about one year old, but I can see right through this baby.

I'm panicking now, and I wake up my girlfriend Roxanne. She immediately says, "What are you doing with those records? Just put them down and go back to sleep." In the morning, she didn't remember about asking me anything about records. How could I see those shadows in my room? There's no reason those shadows should have been there. I just can't figure it out.

A trip to to Bootleggers Supper Club
Tomahawk

Brian followed the trail to Bootleggers Supper Club in Tomahawk, Wisconsin and met up once again with Cory Guessler, who hit the trail, and was now tending bar at Bootleggers. The name of the bar is a clue to the history of the place. Legend has it that it was built by Al Capone in the 1920's. An owner's grandson was paid $1 per day to "watch out for the feds." The place was a halfway mark between Chicago and the Canadian border. The property had been a resort with a stable, and other buildings. It was known as "Phil's place" and was a staple in the Tomahawk community.

So, what's the story at Bootleggers, Cory?

When I go downstairs, I get a real creepy feeling—worse than at the Bar Next Door in Madison. This place is also three times bigger. Alicia, girlfriend of the current cook, rented the upstairs apartment, but she moved out because of the experience that she had. Her little daughter kept crawling into bed with her at night. This was not characteristic behavior for the little girl. Alicia told her daughter that she must sleep in her own bed, but the little girl continued with wanting to crawl into bed with her mother every night. Alicia finally decided to ask her daughter why she was doing this. The little girl said that there was a lady in her room. Finally, after several months of this battle, Alicia was fed up and firmly stated that there was no lady in the girl's bedroom. Then Alicia saw it—an apparition of a woman appeared and faded. Alicia and her daughter moved out the next week. People have seen the woman with the white dress go through the dinning room downstairs from the apartment.

In another incident, the driver of a snowplow who was plowing the lot at around 9 A.M. one morning said that the entire time he was plowing; there was a man in the window of the dinning room watching him. When the plowing job was completed, the man disappeared. During the summer, a couple employees rented the upstairs apartment and had a tough time sleeping due to the constant pacing in the hallway at night. One summer the grandson of previous owner, Phil, stopped in and said that he thought the ghost might be Phil, because his grandfather paced a lot. Things fall off shelves in the kitchen for no apparent reason. The bar has a buzzer that it uses for the kitchen, and this went off by itself on Halloween. It hasn't happened since then. The ghost is called "Old Phil" and everyone thought he was just having some fun buzzing for maybe fifteen seconds.

Waitress Pam recently moved to Tomahawk. She's a very educated person, and she said to me "Cory, I have to tell you everyone is making fun of me because I heard this laughing in the bathroom last Saturday. It was loud and clear. I turned around and there was nobody else in that bathroom." I asked her if perhaps the noise came from the barroom. Pam said, "No. I know how sound travels, and this was as if somebody was behind me, and laughing in my ear. If it were coming from the barroom, it would be muffled." The next night Pam heard the same laughter in the same area, and it was near closing time. The voice was crystal clear, and nobody else was in the bathroom. Pam and another waitress watched the back of the place for at least ten minutes, and nobody came out of the bathroom.

One last word from Cory...

Two of the bartenders and one of the cooks were closing the place up one night. The three were sitting at the bar, and a cold air blast shot through them all. They just sat there silently in shock, you might say. Personally, I have not experienced anything in this establishment yet. I've seen photos with orbs, but I don't hold a lot of faith in that because of dust in the air. Something has come up on EVP (electronic voice phenomenon) I've been told.

Kristin Parker talks about Bootleggers

This used to be Phil's Supper Club, and it is located near Lake Nokomis. If you go down to the basement, you can see "air vents" going out near the windows. This was said to be a lookout for the gangsters. So, there is a history here. Personally, nothing has happened to me here, but I've heard of incidents from other people. When I first took the job, I didn't know about the ghost and the haunt. I wasn't into it. I heard about a woman in white. The bartender who was living here experienced this ghostly woman sitting at his feet, so he moved out. The last tenant who lived here has a daughter who saw the ghost follow the tenant's brother down the hall. The cook saw the ghostly woman moving behind the bar, and the cook was apparently mesmerized. I've heard there is a cat ghost around too.

Do you believe in ghosts? Why do you think people believe in ghosts?

I guess I never did until my husband woke me up one night, and said, "Did you see that!" I wondered how I could have possibly seen anything since I was sleeping at the time. He said, "There was something over you." He had seen an apparition. I haven't seen anything, but there are just too many people out there seeing things to discount it all. You hear so much about it, and people start believing in it. They possibly wish these kinds of things were true.

I don't bother them, and they don't bother me...
— **Bill Kluka, owner of Bootleggers**

We took over the place in August 2001, and I've heard a collection of stories that it was owned by a number of other people through its history. It was built in the 1920's or 1930's and owned by Phil. His grandson is still around. A stairway out in the lobby went down to the basement, and I've heard a bunker or a root cellar existed near the shore. When this was a resort, seventeen cottages were built. As far as ghosts go, it's hard to say. I don't know if the place is haunted or not. I'm here all day, and I don't bother anybody, so I figure any ghost won't bother me either.

The stories say that Phil haunts the place. One of the bartenders was renting upstairs, and he complained that his roommate kept pacing the hall. The roommate was either sound asleep, or not there at all that night. But practical jokers have had their fun too. One of the waitresses might set up a table, and then as a joke, somebody else would "un-set" it, or a waitress would light a candle, and someone else would blow it out. A waitress's friend dropped her off here one evening on her way to work. When the friend came back to pick up the waitress later that night, the friend decided to come in, since she had never been inside here before. The friend said that when she pulled up, there was a woman looking out the window from upstairs. The upstairs is all gutted out, but it used to be apartments up there. When the friend saw the pictures on the dinning room wall, which are supposed to be original, she pointed to one of the women's pictures and said, "That's her!"

Is there any event that occurred here that might prompt

Bootleggers Supper Club in Tomahawk is reportedly haunted by "Phil" and an unknown woman in an upstairs apartment. (Photo by Brian Borton)

a haunting?

No, other than Phil's death, I don't know of anything. I've heard people say that they've heard creaking noises as if a rocking chair were rocking. I guess Phil liked his rocking chair. Some people have been coming here since they were teenagers, and many return here because it's "Phil's place." They think he's still around here, just in a different form.

Janet "Bunny" Kluka talks...

Definitely, this was a bootlegging place from the gangster era. Dillinger and Al Capone hung out here. It was a good size resort, and there were several tunnels. A mother, her daughters and her sister ran the place at one time. There were also rooms upstairs, a carriage house, and things like that. I've heard about footsteps in the hallway, and the last tenant and her nine-year-old daughter experienced things. I've never felt anything. Others sitting at the bar occasionally feel a cold rush of air. Phil loved the place, and he's still here. Yes, I personally think it is haunted. A dog comes in and seems to detect something, but I don't know if it's paranormal or not.

I don't know if any paranormal researchers have checked the place out. I think people are interested in ghosts because it's out of the norm, and that's the thing. It's the weirdness of it all. My own family has had some experiences.

A Terrorized Cat

I was out on an interview trip and talked to a patron at Bootleggers Supper Club, when another patron chirped up and says, "That's nothing compared to what I've been through!" I thought, well, okay; let's hear what you have to say. You know, it kind of perked my attention.

"So, what's been going on?" I said. He said that it all started about seven years ago when he and his fiancé, who is now his wife, were living in an apartment. They started to hear noises, and at first didn't think anything of it—ignored it. Then they began to notice that objects in their apartment were moved. Things were misplaced or put in some unexpected place. You know, you still want to ignore that kind of stuff, and just chock it up to imagination. It became annoying and bothersome, because it was unexplainable. Things were getting too weird.

We had a kitten that was maybe about six months old. One night we invited some friends over, and the five of us were sitting around the family room. All of a sudden, the cat had its tail end pointing away from the couch, and had its face and nose underneath the couch. This hide-a-bed couch had a clearance of about five inches underneath it. The kitten was hissing and clawing at something underneath the couch.

Now, all of the people in the room saw this. We were paying attention because the kitten reacted so strongly with this hissing. All of a sudden, the cat's back end was forcefully whipped around so the back end was underneath the couch. You could see the drag marks from the kitten's claws! The kitten was just screaming at this point, and trying to get away from whatever it was. Then the cat is dragged completely underneath the couch and was just freaking out scared to death. You can see the claw marks in the carpeting where the cat was struggling to get away.

We watched all of this, and nobody wanted to go near that couch. This went on close to thirty seconds before "IT" let the cat go. The cat never went into that family room again—avoided it like the plague. That was the last straw. We moved up north, far away from it.

Another incident happed to the couple sometime later after they had moved. They had a child, and were listening to the baby monitor one night, and they heard a woman's voice and then a little kid's voice. Their baby was only four or five months old, so could not talk, but they could clearly hear a child's voice and a woman's voice. Sometimes a baby monitor can pick up extraneous things, but the couple found it to be very strange and worrisome. Did something follow them?

Another Guest at the Party
Brian talks about his own experience

Ten years ago, I was part of the Madrigals group in school. There were twenty of us, and we decided to go out one night after a practice, and do some partying. So we decided to hang out at a cemetery in Sun Prairie. The land is halfway between Sun Prairie and Columbus. The cemetery is supposedly haunted, but we weren't out looking for any ghostly guests for the party. We got there, and then we had another 15 people with us. The cemetery is small. There's a wooded area, a road and a cornfield. I and five other people saw a little girl in a white dress. She looked like she was three to five years old. The apparition came out of the woods, hovered at the corner of the cemetery, and then disappeared in the cornstalks. She was actually translucent.

I know for a fact that I saw this, and five other people did too. You could see right through her, and I think this is what frightened us. We didn't run out; we had so many people there, but it kind of wigged us out. I heard stories from other people about this particular apparition, but I never expected personally to run into her. The only thing out that way besides the cemetery was a farmhouse at the time.

A Dog named Hello?

About a year and a half ago, around 10 PM, my husband Jeff and I were watching the TV show *Everybody Loves Raymond*, and we were both lying in bed. I had just turned on the TV, and the volume was not all the way up yet. Then, all of a sudden, we heard a male voice, like an older sounding gentleman. The voice said, "Hello? Hello?" It almost sounded like my grandfather. It sounded like someone was opening the front door, and it was as if someone was saying "hello" in such a way that they were meaning, "Hello? Is anybody home?" It was as if a neighbor might be popping in to visit.

The only reason that I halfway acknowledged it is because my husband whipped around and looked at me just as fast as I turned and looked at him. Jeff is not into paranormal or any of that stuff. He teases me all the time about it, calls my mom a gypsy, and things like that. But this time, Jeff was so convinced somebody was in the house that he had me grab the kids. He took the bat that he keeps under the bed and then he went downstairs. We ended up calling the police. They came and checked inside and outside, and thought we were nuts. This happened in late fall, and the windows were all shut. But, nonetheless Jeff said, "Oh, it must have been the neighbors calling the dog."

I said, "Since when did the neighbors name their dog 'Hello'?"

The weirdest thing that happened though was the following week when I found a silver ring in the bedroom. It was on the floor and under a box near my bookshelf. This was very strange. I had never before seen it in my life. It was like a sterling silver saddle-type of ring. I gave it to my Aunt Paula who has always had a close connection with horses and riding. Nobody in the family had ever seen the ring before. Paula still has it. To this day, my husband acknowledges that the incident with the voice happened, and he certainly remembers it vividly, but he still tries to explain it away. We slept with the lights on that night. We slept with the TV on too. He still wants to sleep with the TV on now. I think he feels it's safer that way, even though he likes to remain skeptical.

Roving Writer Brian Asks, "Do you believe in ghosts?"

Do you believe in ghosts? Why do you think people have a desire to believe?

.......**Well, kind of**. Why? People are afraid they are going to die and nothing else is going to be left.

.......**No,** I don't believe in ghosts. I think people have a need for the mental illusion—sort of a mental opiate.

.......**Absolutely**, I believe in ghosts. Why is there a need? Is there a need because they have actually experienced the phenomenon? A friend of mine just got out of jail, and she had a lot of anger. As I was watching her, I saw this old woman's face. It was somebody else's face. I told this spirit that she could leave that body now. Then my friend's face changed. Actually, I see ghosts on occasion, especially in alcoholics and people who are angry. The people seem to attract these sorts of energy. They open themselves up to it.

.......**Yes,** I believe in ghosts. Why? It's because people already believe that people go to a different place when they die. So, if you don't believe that a soul is destroyed, and that soul does not go to a heaven or hell, they probably just float around and hang around the living I suppose.

.......**Ya,** I think there's something to all this. There's a house called Windy Willows, or something like that [author note: probably refers to Summerwind Mansion]. When they dug the ground to build the house, there were Indian burial grounds there. A mansion was built, but nobody was able to inhabit it. The place burned two or three years ago. Someone wanted to turn it into a restaurant and hotel inn. No one had inhabited it for at least twenty years. They'd paint rooms, and then they'd come back the next day, and the rooms would be back to looking the way they did seventy years ago—paint peeling, things like that.

The government actually studied it a couple of years ago. I went there as a child a few times, and I couldn't go in the place. There was some sort of barrier, and the hair on the back of my neck just stood up. There's another place around Lacrosse, I think. The foundation of the house is left. It's in a wooded area. If you go in there, you'll experience wind and cold if you step inside the foundation of the house, even if it is a warm and calm day. The house was supposedly struck by lightening, but maybe some of the locals just burned it down because they didn't want people going back there.

.......**I think it is quite possible**. Why should we discount something for which nobody has a definite answer? Every culture has its myths, but myths, more often than not, are based on actual events. Although a myth has that wonderful creative quality about it that reality sometimes does not have. I believe people are optimistic at a gut level. And if there is a spirit world, then perhaps there is optimism that a heaven or other such place is home to the soul.

.......**Certainly!** Hey, everybody gets invited to the party. Why exclude people just because they might be in a different form now! It's okay to be skeptical, but let's not close any door—that's just plain stupid. There's a lot to learn out in the world, and nobody has the answers to it all, and especially to this stuff!

Cinnamon Toast

Do you believe in ghosts, Judy of Adams County?
I am a firm believer in ghosts. I say that because of my
own experiences with the paranormal. I grew up in a house in
Wausau, Wisconsin. My family would occasionally see Aunt
Barbara walking into the kitchen from her bedroom. Aunt
Barbara died of tuberculosis long before there was any cure
for it. She used the rocking chair in her bedroom a lot. The
rocking chair remained in place after she died. There have
been several times when that chair has rocked for six to eight
hours at a time. But these are merely the minor incidents that
I've had with what I consider ghostly phenomenon. Another
memorable experience happened while I was living in Illinois.
You recognize the smell of cinnamon toast, don't you?

Every day at 3:00 P.M, and I mean *every* day, the pleasant
aroma of cinnamon toast would fill this very large house,
known as the Reidy House, where we living in Lisle, Illinois.
The house was very old, and had a rather unique and interesting history. It was the first house of magnitude, you might
say, that was in this town. The family was prominent, owned
a lumber mill, and so on. They had a lot of influence.

The house had five bedrooms upstairs, a very large attic
with room enough to stand, a living room, sunroom, kitchen,
dinning room, and music room. After the original owners
left, the house became a convent owned by the Catholic
Church. One of the nuns, Sister Catherine, was a daughter
of the former owner of the house. The house had also been
a rectory for the Catholic Church. Eventually, the house
went on the market and an East Indian couple bought it as
rental property.

One batch of renters had been drug runners, and the
DEA (drug enforcement) made a raid and shut down the
operation. In doing so, the agents kicked in the back door
by the kitchen. The damaged door was replaced with a new
door. When my family rented the Reidy House, we noticed

that the door looked different from the rest of the house. A very large old oak tree near the house had a limb sawed off, and plain as day, you could see the perfect image of a nun in the place where the limb had been. I remember when my sister-in-law came to visit. She drove up in her car, came into the house, and the first thing she said was, "My God, did you see that tree?"

I knew she must have been referring to the image, so I told her that we call the nun Sister Catherine. But what's really very curious, and very interesting is the fact that the nun image stares directly at the replaced kitchen door, as if she is watching and guarding the place. We also noticed that the more work we did on the house to restore it and maintain it, the more the nun faded out, as if she could lessen her watch duty because someone was helping.

This house had a rich ambiance about it. It had oil gas light fixtures that were converted to electric. We lived in the house for five years, and there was never any time that my family felt fearful or threatened in any way. We believed that it could be haunted, but it never bothered us. It struck me as strange when we were first considering renting the old house, and the owner said, "Don't believe in any of those ghost stories you might hear." It was as if he were trying to push something under the rug—minimize any rumor damage.

Whoever or whatever was there, we felt that the entities had a gentle presence about "them." One night I heard a group of people talking in the music room, but there was nobody in that area, and the lights were off. I went to check it out anyhow, and I saw that the light above the piano was on. Another incident happened when my daughter put my grandson, Matt, down for a nap in his crib in the nursery. We began to hear a lot of giggling and laughing. When we checked on him, we could see the mobile above the crib was moving. Matt was gazing at something next to the crib, but we could not see what it was. My daughter said that as she walked into the room she felt a nightgown swish across her legs.

I don't know what it's like for anybody who lives there now, but I also believe that to experience some of these things, a person has to be "in tune" with it. Certainly, it would be easy to just go about your business, be oblivious to subtle occurrences, and basically miss amazing things that could be happening all around you. Yes, I firmly believe in ghosts whether they bring with them cinnamon toast or not.

Highway O

Do you believe in ghosts?
Yes, I do. There is a house on Highway O. It's built on top of an Indian cemetery, and I think next to it is another cemetery. The house has little square room that is like a four-foot high box. When you're in that room, it feels like somebody is touching you, but nobody is there. Lights turn on in that house and nobody is there. People have heard footsteps and doors opening.

Do you believe in ghosts?
I never used to think much about it until something happened. My dad and I were driving past an old graveyard one night after a junior high wrestling tournament. It was a very dark night, cloudy, no moon. I noticed a glowing figure in the field next to the graveyard on my side of the road. It was about 100 yards away from a house. I asked dad to slow down so we could get a better look. We still have no explanation for what we saw that night.

A Tired Ghost

Do you believe in ghosts?
I think I do, or at least I'm open to the possibility. When

I was seven or eight, I was sleeping on the second floor of the house in a back room. In the middle of the night, a white figure wearing a white nightgown crawled into bed between my sister and me. The figure was of an older woman. I was so scared, I couldn't scream. I just froze. That's the best way I can put it. I never said anything to my sister all those years. And then decades later, my sister all of a sudden says, "You saw that lady too." My sister saw the lady more than once. If it was a ghost, she seemed to have form. My sister said that when she saw the lady, she was not scared, and tried to tell herself it was our grandmother. She knew it wasn't. Grandma was still alive at the time.

Reflections

Do you believe in ghosts?

Yes, I do believe in spirits. Every Sunday I had lunch with my mother. One time I decided to bring my camera and take a few pictures. When I had the photos developed, we could clearly see the reflection of my father in the TV set. He had been deceased for years. Another photo showed him as a reflection in the patio door.

Charlie

Do you believe in ghosts?

It's possible. I worked in a county nursing home. It was a very old building, and part of it had been made into four home units. One night I was working, and had two nursing assistants with me that night. Both of them went on a break, and I went to check on the residents. I was astonished to find bedpans lined all the way down the hallway! Immediately, I concluded it was a joke. But thinking back, it would have been impossible for anybody to pull this off without my knowing. The aids had gone to break and had not been in that part of the building at all. Then I heard that it must be "Charlie." I guess Charlie walks around the building at night, and he has been haunting the place for a long time. Another time there were towels all the way down the handrails.

I've never seen Charlie, but strange things happen in the place. I think he's harmless, just odd.

Animal Encounters with the Paranormal and Paranormal Animals R Us

We usually think of ghosts as entities related to human form. Like other places on the planet, Wisconsin has its stock of animal ghostly form. Wisconsin legend gives us ghosts of horses, dogs, wolves, and coyote. Often times, a cat is reported in spectral settings. One account even includes a ghostly owl. Aside from animal ghosts, we have ghosts that seem to gain the attention of various living animals, most commonly cats and dogs and horses. Birds play a significant role in mythology, cosmology, in foreshadowing events, and in the delivery of messages. We ran across one tale of a mysterious bird coming to the rescue in a vengeful storm. Was it a spirit, or perhaps a helpful ghost? Cows, ghostly or not, seem to take a spotlight in Wisconsin too.

What's Wisconsin without a few ghostly cows?

A curious account comes from famed Folklorist Dennis Boyer. He writes about the Lime Ridge cows of Sauk County in his wonderful book *Driftless Spirits*. We're not quite sure when these cows started trudging down the road, but apparently no reports of this surfaced before 1957. On one of the Dennis Boyer outings, he came across a resident purveyor of such oddities in a Loganville café.

According to the local coffee connoisseur, the entire herd is composed of Brown Swiss cows, much to the dismay of Holstein fanciers. In fact, the old timers say, the appearance of the Brown Swiss are just a form of protest against the competitive Holsteins. Until we read this, we didn't realize cows paid much attention to bovine ethnicity. Mr. Coffee remarked about how the countryside really was a colorful patchwork quilt of many different breeds of livestock, pig, sheep, horses, and poultry. This was a time when not all cows were black and white.

So what about these Brown Swiss cows? The herd consists of about two dozen cows, which was an average size herd for a farm of the 1940's or 1950's. The cows walk in single file along the road at night. Nobody knows whose herd that might have been.

A final word from Mr. Coffee about the nighttime cows...

Don't think that doesn't throw off some drivers. The drunks are lucky.

They just drive through the cow ghosts, and blink their eyes. The sober drivers often swerve and damage their cars. One old fellow tried to put their wanderings to an end. He tried to leave them to an abandoned barn in the area. But the cows bulked at the door. My theory is that those cows are waiting for things to get straightened out. When we get back to a country life that works, then those cows will go home.

(Quoted from *Driftless Spirits* (1996) by Dennis Boyer)

Wren in bad weather...

When (or in this case "wren") you hit a stint of nature's furry in the form of a fierce snowstorm, what do you do? Probably the last thing on your mind is bird watching for the day. The impact of winter in Door County is not to be taken lightly. The surrounding waters and nor'easter winds dance dangerously with the blinding snow. One year in January, a narrow strip of water remained open between Washington Island and the Northport pier, but the ferry schedule had been severely reduced. Hermie, who ran the ferry and his friend Judd decided to take a jaunt over to the mainland to have a day of fun. Judd thought he should probably invite Frieda, Hermie's wife along, but she declined. Hermie had been complaining that Frieda had been buying too much corn to feed the birds. He remarked that Frieda would probably not want to go to the same places they were going to hit that day, but he would bring her back some fabric that she had been wanting for new kitchen curtains.

Hermie and Judd set out in the morning to follow the track across the ice to Ellison Bay. The gale force wind had diminished overnight, and huge snowdrifts now dotted the area. White cedars were cut around the first of the year and then placed in holes dug in the ice to form a reliable car track from the island to the mainland. The two men started out in Judd's car heading westward away from the treacherous ice of the Door where a person could be on safe ice one minute, and then caught on an ice floe the next, or plunged into the mighty cold waters.

The two friends ran errands, stopped at the Ellison Bay store to buy nails and curtain material, and drank and talked their way through lunch. The clouds would be moving in soon. And with that came the possibility of uncertain weather, so Judd and Hermie were planning to start their journey back home. They ran into another friend who invited them for a drink. Not wanting to appear unfriendly, and always up for another round of socializing, the trio continued longer than planned on their outing. At dusk, they finally pulled the black Model-T type Ford onto the ice at Ellison Bay. Snow was lightly falling, but they thought the task of heading home would be unencumbered because they'd simply follow the tree-lined track across the ice to the island.

Sometimes, light snow can be deceiving. The snowfall

started playing a little rougher, and soon the car's headlights had a hard time keeping up with visibility. Suddenly, the car ran right into a snowdrift. Hermie and Judd hopped out of the car, but couldn't budge it forward or backward. Judd thought he could see the lights of Washington Island, so the two travelers decided to hike it on foot and abandon the car. In a matter of minutes, they lost sight of the car and of the line of trees. Snow whipped around, causing the hikers to lose sense of direction. They could barely see three feet in front of them. The danger was that they could be walking into the Door onto thin ice and an open channel of water. The dilemma was that if they stayed, they might freeze in a mater of a couple of hours, but if they continued, the outcome was even more uncertain.

Judd and Hermie began to walk staying within arms length of each other. They stopped to rest when Hermie, who questioned whether he was hallucinating, saw a bird. He asked Judd if he saw the bird, and Judd just shook his head and said that it would be impossible for a bird to be out there on a stormy night like this. Hermie insisted that the bird was right at about waist high. He tugged on Judd to turn around and look. Sure enough, Judd saw the bird. "Looks like a wren to me, but those are summer birds. None of those birds around here in the winter," said Judd.

Hermie then remarked that Frieda puts up wren houses, but seeing a wren in the winter wasn't going to happen. Nonetheless, the little bird stayed slightly ahead of the travelers, but in sight if they were careful enough to watch. They followed the bird. It seemed to be leading them, and if they veered off the path, the bird would disappear until they found their way again. Through drifts and blowing snow, the men followed the bird until they could see the lights of the Johannson place at Detroit Harbor. They knew they could make it now.

Then the bird disappeared. Judd worried about the wren's departure. There was just no sign of the bird that lead them to safety, and away from perilous waters, and freezing to death. Judd and Hermie ended up at the Johannson's place and told their story about the bird before getting a ride home from the family. The next day, Hermie was busy repainting Frieda's old wren house and building another one for the next summer. He no longer complained about bread and corn for the birds.

Horse's disapproval

We heard another story from Ephraim on the Door County peninsula. Around the turn of the century, late 1800s, a particular merchant named Jack had a habit of Sunday fishing taking the place of Sunday going to church. The wife frowned on this since she'd dress the kids up every week and dutifully attend the services. It so happened, that the Reverend was rounding the bend one day in his horse and buggy, when he came upon Jack, whose horse and wagon were stalled. The horse was just going nowhere, no matter how much coaxing, whip cracking, or colorful commands Jack attempted to use.

The Reverend, patient and wise man that he was, greeted Jack and instantly noted that Jack was in a troublesome position. The Reverend also noted that the wagon was not carrying a heavy load. He then inquired if something had frightened the horse, or was he just acting up today. Jack said it was strange because he thought maybe some rabbits had run across his path and perhaps this spooked the horse, but that in the past, this never bothered the horse. The Reverend got down off his buggy and took a look at the horse and a look around the wagon.

"Jack," said the Reverend, "Your problem is that you're carrying an extra passenger that your horse disapproves of." Confused, Jack thought the Reverend probably needed glasses. But the Reverend persisted and said that Lucifer, the devil was sitting in the back of the wagon, and that Jack's horse was going nowhere until this all cleared out. The Reverend made Jack a deal. He said he'd get rid of the devil if Jack would show up in church on Sundays. Jack, not knowing how to get rid of a devil, decided to accept this deal. So the Reverend got out his well-worn Bible and began to read in a couple of places. He then went back to Jack and told him the horse was all set to go, and the unwanted passenger was gone. Horse and driver continued on their journey, and horse and driver attended church the next Sunday for several months thereafter. Apparition, devil, spirit, ghost, stubborn horse?

Big pig exorcism

Another tale discovered by Dennis Boyer for his book *Driftless Spirits* tells us of the Vernon County five-hundred-pound boar hog who was "possessed." as they say. The hog was unburdened of this ghostly possession by a self-proclaimed exorcist in Hillsboro. This story has a Lake Woebegone flavor about it. The boar hog had a territory around Cox Creek and had an appetite for poultry, dogs, and cats. Folks were beginning to worry that the children might be next.

The local exorcist, a grandfather who saw little in life that was not in need of healing, planned to hang a crucifix around the neck of the boar. Fat chance. The exorcist made his move, only to have the wild guy take off on a two mile ride with the clinging Exorcist Grandpa in tow. Not giving up by a long shot, Exorcist Grandpa pressed the crucifix chain into the boar's neck cutting off the oxygen supply long enough to force the racing hog to take a time-out, so to speak. It's been said that after the rampage, the hog was a true Christian.

Exorcist Grandpa was a handy person to have around the house. He studied rituals and spells. His work included ridding many a house, church, stable, blacksmith shop, and barn of ghosts and evil, not that the two are related. Amongst other outstanding feats, he was able to take care of a cursed nail that soured the milk in a particular barn.

Pogo the watchdog detects Captain Gust

One of the legends coming out of Door County is of Captain Gust. He was considered fairly sociable, and liked to attend dinner at the house he allegedly haunts. The Captain was born in Sweden and named Gustav Anders. He became a ship Captain for the Great Lakes Line, and settled for a time in Door County where he built a large house on Washington Island. He and wife, Anna, raised a family. Captain Gust was a likeable fellow with a sense of humor. He loved laughter and music. Eventually, the family moved to Milwaukee, and then to California.

Later day owners of the house suspect that the Captain is back. When new owners moved in and started to unpack their belongings, it seems that the ghost wasted little time in making his presence known. As Betty was unpacking some towels upstairs, she heard a friendly laugh coming from the bottom of the stairs. Thinking that a neighbor had stopped by to welcome her family to the neighborhood, she went downstairs to greet the person. Pogo the terrier wasn't quite as accepting of the situation. The pooch stood in the center of the dinning room barking and growling at the bay windows.

Betty searched the house and found nobody. The laughter continued sporadically over the next few months. The ghost was more active after the family bought a piano. Remember, Captain Gust liked laughter and music. Now he had both. Betty and her husband Jack awoke one night and heard plunking on the piano. At first, they thought one of the kids was playing a late night sonata. Pogo, sleeping at the end of the bed, woke up and raced down the hallway, barking every step of the way. The couple dashed to the dinning room and found Pogo barking at the piano stool.

You might think this would be a one-time occurrence, and everyone could get on with life. Not so. The piano playing occurred so frequently over the next few months, that even Pogo didn't bother to get up to check it out. The months stretched into several years of piano notes. But the ghost story doesn't end there.

Betty placed an antique rocker in front of the bay windows. She began to notice that when the family ate at the table, the rocking chair would rock just slightly. The family decided it was probably air currents or something plausible, but Pogo disagreed.

Weeks after the acquisition of the rocking chair, Betty noticed a faint image of a human form in the chair. The apparition took on more detail, and soon both Betty and her daughter were able to see the Captain smiling and rocking. Betty's husband and her son could only see the chair rocking, and not the Captain's image.

Pogo never adjusted to the ghostly visitor, and barked whenever Captain Gust was present. Apparently, this sociable ghost would sit quietly in the rocking chair listening to dinner conversations when there were guests in the house. Seventeen years after the family moved into the house, they extensively remodeled the kitchen, and painted the dining room and living rooms. They rearranged the furniture and closed down a back stairway. Captain Gust disappeared after this, and the owners remarked that they rather missed him.

Peanut the raccoon
still eats those sandwiches

Raccoons can be mighty persistent characters. My brother and I had a raccoon when we were growing up, and it became obvious to us that these are creatures of set-in-stone habit—a time to eat, a time to sleep, and a time to wander on into the house to watch a TV program, and always, always, always be sure to take advantage of hand-outs. Egg Harbor had a raccoon so appropriately named

"Peanut" who, you may guess, had a voracious appetite for the delicacy known as peanut butter sandwich. The story starts with Miss Emma, a schoolteacher living in Egg Harbor who taught at many of the one-room schoolhouses. She took in stray animals, and her career as a teacher ended when she married Oscar. Some say that Oscar was another one of those strays, but nonetheless the couple was married for forty years. Schoolteachers in those days were generally single ladies, since married women were not considered suitable for the job.

Before they were married, Miss Emma had hired Oscar to shingle the leaky roof on her cottage. He was able to get half the shingling done, when he slipped on the ladder and broke an ankle. Miss Emma, of course, used to taking in and mending the strays of the world, took in Oscar while she finished shingling the roof. It was improper to have a young man living at the house of a young unmarried woman in those days. The two married, and solved that particular problem.

Miss Emma's place became a stray-a-thon. Battle-worn cats and adventurous dogs found refuge and food at the back steps of the cottage. Injured birds were revived, and squirrels eagerly plucked peanuts that had been laid out on the windowsills. A lame cow even roamed over to stay at the shed, refusing to return home. Oscar didn't mind all this animal company. But the peanuts opened another chapter for the couple, and caused disagreement. Oscar grew peanuts in this inhospitable ground and climate. Nobody has figured out how he was able to do that, since the ground was more rock than soil. Yet year after year, he proudly cultivated the generous crop.

One bumper crop year, Miss Emma had the idea to try out a new approach to using peanuts. She read something about it in a magazine the year before, but could not recall the recipe, so she improvised. Miss Emma ground up the peanuts, and mixed them with other ingredients. She spread the peanut experiment on a piece of bread and served it to Oscar for lunch. They both agreed that the recipe was not up to speed, unfit for consumption according to Oscar. Miss Emma stayed with the task and finally produced a recipe that Oscar loved. His standard lunch became a peanut butter sandwich.

A young raccoon, minding his own business, wandered into the yard. But one of the dogs not familiar with Miss Emma's rule of no nasty behavior chased the raccoon up an electric pole. The baby raccoon touched some of the hot spots, which sent jolts of electricity through his little body. Fur stood on end, and the poor raccoon fell to the ground. Oscar ran from the barn to see what had happened. Miss Emma scooped the frazzled and fried raccoon up in her arms and ran to the kitchen. She was disgusted with the new-fangled thing called "electricity."

The severely injured raccoon was nursed back to health. Miss Emma forced the little animal to drink teaspoons of milk. She carefully tended the burns, and by the end of the summer, the healthy raccoon had become a pampered pet. The cost of the electric pole ordeal was a right ear and a couple of toes on his right foot. Mischief progressed in proportion to the little coon's recovery. To Oscar's dismay, the young raccoon repeatedly climbed the tree, and then couldn't quite figure out how on earth he was going to reach ground level again. "I think that electricity addled his brain. What's that dang fool climbing a tree for if he can't get down?" said Oscar. "That coon's more trouble than all the rest put together!"

Miss Emma, always a woman who firmly had her say in matters, scolded Oscar, and said he was out of sorts because she made them take that pole away. "We don't want that kind of thing here half killing innocent animals." In Oscar's world, the only good that came from having this raccoon around was the fact that the critter loved the early peanut butter recipe failures that Miss Emma had concocted and test-drove on Oscar.

Well, as you might guess, things didn't end there. The raccoon, now appropriately named "Peanut," worked his way through all the peanut butter reject jars from the root cellar. Peanut wasn't fussy, he could move on to the good stuff without hesitation. So, before you know it, reluctant Oscar had to share the best peanut butter with comrade Peanut. Both Oscar and Peanut had peanut butter sandwiches daily for lunch. It was an entertaining time in itself. The peanut butter would stick to the roof of the raccoon's mouth, and he'd go through all kinds of acrobatics, including somersaulting off the cabinet, which resulted in this furry ball of a raccoon landing with a thud on the floor.

Oscar's complaints continued as Peanut took himself shopping in Oscar's garden. One time Oscar complained that the raccoon had stripped three ears of corn and didn't eat any of it. Miss Emma said that it wasn't necessarily Peanut doing the deed. It could have been any number of creatures wandering about. Oscar replied that there aren't that many right-footed two-toed raccoons out there leaving footprints in the mud. Emma said she'd have a little chat with Peanut.

On that same day, Miss Emma sent Oscar to the root cellar for a jug of cider, figuring the cool tart cider would help tame Oscar's annoyance with Peanut. Oscar came up from the cellar and spotted muddy footprints of one raccoon in particular that lead across the kitchen floor, over the kitchen table, and ended at Oscar's chair where there, sitting perched on the chair, was Peanut. Now it was about lunchtime, and it probably seemed pretty logical that Peanut would be nibbling. Peanut was sitting on his hind legs, holding a sandwich is his front paws, and savoring every bite. Oscar commented that he wouldn't have any rest until that dang fool coon was gone. Wrong.

To Oscar's credit, after many years of putting up with garden raids and peanut butter sandwich snatching, Peanut died a natural death, and Oscar respectfully buried Peanut. About a week later when Miss Emma was going in to town, she left a sandwich out for Oscar, same as usual. He came into the house after working on the bean plants in the garden, and noticed that half his sandwich was gone. Oscar grumbled about Miss Emma eating half the sandwich, but scratched his head a little on this one, since Miss Emma was not fond of peanut butter. The half-eaten sandwich event repeated itself several times over in the ensuing months. Oscar and Miss Emma argued about it, with Oscar blaming Miss Emma, and Miss Emma saying she wasn't the culprit because she preferred butter and jam.

Then one day, it happened. Oscar came into the kitchen after working the large garden. It had rained the night before and he removed his boots to avoid tracking mud across the clean kitchen floor. He glanced at the table to see what was for lunch. Miss Emma's plate had a cheese sandwich. Oscar's plate had the customary peanut butter sandwich with a large bite nibbled out of the side. Tracking across the floor was the evidence—raccoon prints with the hind right foot having only two toes.

Miss Emma quit making peanut butter sandwiches ahead of time, because invariably if she did, a chunk of the sandwich would be missing due to some invisible raccoon force. Oscar and Miss Emma had no more quarrels about the sandwiches, and Oscar would merely cut around the raccoon bite marks if he happened to get a partial sandwich that day.

Supposedly, the raccoon continued to help himself to unattended peanut butter sandwiches long after Emma and Oscar had departed the little cottage and new owners had taken over. Little tiffs over who took a bite out of my peanut butter sandwich continued for years. I think this whole collection of events has something to do with Oscar's blasted new fangled electric pole and the electro-zap incident of a little Peanut.

(Information: Ghosts of Door County Wisconsin (1992) by Geri Rider).

Transparent Chickens

Chicken Alley has a weirdly appealing name to it. It's the kind of place you'd find in say Seymour, Shawano County, Maple Grove Township, Up North, Wisconsin. Well, it's not in your imagination. It's actually a place on the map. Somehow, I picture this chicken hide-away where the birds are all sitting around a table playing poker like the poker-playing dogs. But since this is a book about ghosts, we're talking about phantom chickens. Chicken Alley is an L-shaped road outside of Shawano. There's really nothing remarkable about it except for the strange name. It's sort of a typical rural Wisconsin road out in the wide-open farm country.

The story goes that witnesses have seen phantom chickens running near the road. These chickens are the usual brand except that the observer can see right through them. And then when you think that you can hardly believe your eyes, the chickens vanish! Probably something better to do in a different dimension, I suppose. But Chicken Alley has a few other mysterious twists to it too. If you park your car, and walk to the intersection of French Road and Chicken Alley, an annoyed voice might yell at you to get out of the road, same way your parents bossed you around when you were trying to ride the tricycle out of the driveway. The Chicken Alley street sign is said to disappear. At other times it's nowhere to be seen.

Then there's the matter of the tree. Supposedly, a large tall gnarly tree guards the side of the road, but the tree is only visible on the night of the full moon, or the tree is not present at all. What would a haunting be without those unexplainable lights? Chicken Alley has that too. Lights in various shapes, sizes, and colors approach at high speed and disappear just as quickly. Some say that during the winter, phantom snowmobiles are on the run, but that just sounds like a detail cooked up on a cold winter night and added to the chicken story. We decided that if you're worried about too many calories, maybe you should check out this place that has transparent chickens.

Fact, Fiction and Legends to Ponder

The book *Famous Wisconsin Ghosts and Ghost Hunters* is primarily about haunting, real and unreal. However, Wisconsin has an exceptionally rich tradition in folklore that blossoms from the seedlings of haunted tales. Anytime there's a story of extremes, it catches our interest. Ghosts live somewhere in that extreme fringe, and thus become the intriguing main characters that they are. But when you think about it, there's not much to a ghost really. The character doesn't say much, the entity is often rather nondescript in appearance, and most of the time it's just there doing nothing.

So what we are truly latching on to is the *story* of something out of the ordinary. The *story* is what peaks our interest and that's what perpetuates legend. And the telling of a story is an art. The Ridgeway Ghost stories have been handed down, embellished, and grown in number since about the 1840's. There seems to be two categories. In the major category, the stories consist mostly of sightings here and there in rural settings, frightening encounters, and vanishing apparitions. A minor category covers the rarer tales that are about imitation ghosts. We've included both kinds of stories here as a break from the more serious haunting, investigative, and "documented" type of ghost encounter.

Ridgeway Ghost:
Spinning a web of tales

In their classic book, *Wisconsin Lore* by Robert E. Gard and L.G. Sorden, the infamous Ridgeway Ghost of Iowa

County commands a prominent and ominous presence. The collection of Ridgeway Ghost tales grows richer with the years, and lives through dark night story telling and various written accounts. This nasty specter changes forms, including animal forms, to fit the situation. The entity has been described in animal shapes as apparitions of pigs, sheep, cows, horses, and dogs. Other forms include that of mysterious strangers, women, and the totally invisible. The Ridgeway ghost claimed its territory over the length of the old Military Road around the Pokerville settlement at Blue Mounds to Dodgeville. The early highway was known as the Ridge Road, and was littered with saloons. Although there are numerous tales of how this all began, a few horrible events are most prominent, and may have triggered an unleashing of the Ridgeway Ghost.

Traveler beware

The first story takes us to Sampson's Saloon and Hotel. The place had a reputation for its lawlessness, as did many of the establishments, and its all round bottom-of-the-pit lack of appeal. Once upon a time, an unsuspecting traveler checked into the Hotel at the end of the day. The traveler disappeared under extremely questionable circumstances. His saddled horse tried to enter the Saloon-Hotel the next day only to be chased away.

Shortly after that unexplained incident, people began to report an incredibly frightening apparition on the road near Sampson's Saloon. It was a black horse carrying a headless horseman sitting backward in the saddle. The terrifying ghost kept pace with or passed travelers on the road, often groaning in suffering moans. Headless horsemen can be found here and there in folklore, and we don't hear much, other than they chase through town, as in Washington Irving's *The Legend of Sleepy Hollow*. But Ridgeway's headless horseman seems to be particularly in a traveling mode, and has been seen on many occasions.

Horse along for the ride

One buggy driver related a tale of fright that actually may have lead to his death shortly afterwards, since it is unknown what became of the driver. The man reported that he was driving his buggy and heard a horse coming up from behind. He turned his head expecting to see the horse either following him, or passing him along the side. There was no headless horseman on this trip, but what he saw was just as unbelievable.

The specter horse reared up and planted its feet squarely in the buggy driver's wagon as the wagon was traveling down the road. The horse's front quarters where merely a few inches from the back of the buggy driver who was terrified by now. The driver sped up his team of horses to outpace the phantom horse, but it didn't work. The phantom kept pace. No one knows what eventually became of the buggy driver, but it's said that he was never the same after that horrific event.

Tragedy in fire and ice

Tragedy has never made any sense. The outcomes often change lives or destroy lives. So goes the story of two young boys in the wrong place at the wrong time. Climb aboard your Way-Back vehicle and travel back to 1840 to the McKillip's tavern five miles west of Ridgeway. Two brothers, ages fourteen and fifteen stopped in the tavern on a very cold winter day. Drunken patrons of the place turned taunting of the boys into violence, used plain stupid judgment, and threw one of the boys in the fire. The boy burned to death. The surviving boy escaped, and ran into the cold and ice of winter. In the spring, the boy's body was found in a field where he had frozen to death. Shortly after the deaths of the two adolescents, a gray-haired woman was seen wandering near McKillip's as if she were in search of something. She would vanish quickly if anybody approached her. The small gray-haired woman has been the topic of other tales in the area. Some say she can be spotted trudging down the road, but disappearing into a ball of fire.

A Woman in Charge

Another tale of the Ridgeway ghost was told by a man who reported driving his team of horses near Ridgeway when he noticed a woman walking down the road ahead of him. She was in the middle of the road traveling in the same direction as the driver and his horses. The driver yelled at the woman to move aside, but she did not respond. She seemed oblivious to the approaching horses. The driver tried to pass the woman on the side, but she moved to block his efforts. He then prodded the horses into a gallop to get past the woman, but she continued to block him. Frustrated, and wondering if he was hallucinating, the driver brought his team of horses to a halt, only to find that the woman halted too. After a few miles of playing this surrealistic game, the woman simply vanished.

Tired Dog

Sometimes dogs get as tired as their owners do, but this particular dog seems to have been tired far beyond his days of chasing in the country. A place called the Reilly House was built near the railroad tracks about five miles west of Ridgeway. The house was built in the late 1800's or early 1900's, and Mr. Peavey lived in the house. After he moved, the house burned down, but a new house was constructed on the original foundation. Apparently, a phantom large black dog decided to move in at that point. The canine appeared under the dining room table every night, tired and panting. The new owners did not approve, and fled the house days later after seeing the dog vanish a few times. The house itself did not seem to be affected, because when the structure was moved to its present location, the dog apparition did not tag along with the house. Some say it stayed with the foundation.

But is the house free of anomalies? Recent residents of the house reported that their young daughter had been frightened by the sound of children playing with marbles that rolled across the floor. The sounds came from the attic, but no explanation for the sound was ever found.

Pig Tales

It seems like the Ridgeway Ghost grows his own farm animals to sizes unheard of in the ordinary world. A story about Mr. Lewis, on his way home from doing some butchering at a local farm, is one of several pig tales. After butchering some animals at a local farm, Lewis was on his way home one evening. He was walking down Ridge Road when he noticed a sow and young pigs barely moving down the road ahead of him. The closer he came to the pigs, the larger they grew. This growth phenomenon was getting out of hand, and by the time he reached the animals, they were as large as cows and getting larger. Not knowing what to do, Lewis struck out at them with his butcher knife, and watched with disbelief as the pigs vanished suddenly. Shortly after this involvement with the ghostly swine, Lewis died. It was said that he could never get over this incident, and that he died because of the frightful experience.

The Pig Exchange

A farmer named George Russell, near Ridgeway had arranged with another farmer to purchase a pig. The two men met in Ridgeway, and the pig was transferred to a crate of the back of George Russell's wagon. After running a few errands, Russell hitched up his horses to the wagon and headed home. After arriving home, he opened the crate to get the pig out, but instead of a pig, out came a rather large dog. Nobody knows exactly what happened here. Did the Ridgeway Ghost arrange a ghostly exchange or was this a joke played on Russell?

Tricky Cards

The Ridgeway ghost likes to play poker, according to a few of those who take to the entertainment. A tale tells of a night that three men were playing cards at a saloon in Pokerville. The three men played several hands, and a pot of money was nicely situated at the center of the table. One of the players won the prize with a full house in his hand. He reached forward to collect his bounty and suddenly an unfamiliar hand reached forward, grabbed the deck of cards, and began dealing.

The cards flew from the strange hand to the table in front of the three players. A stranger had taken the vacant seat at the table. He had a hat pulled partly over his face. The cards dealt from the hand of the stranger performed all kinds of tricks as he cast them to the table. If another player tried to pick up a card, the card would escape the player and fly around the room. This had to be a problem, especially when much of the deck had taken to circling the room.

The astonished poker players departed rather quickly, running into each other as they left. It is said that even the door was left hanging by its hinges because the men were so eager to escape the room. The stranger fourth poker player, along with the pot of money, disappeared. The bartender, it was told, hid out behind the bar and consumed a large quantity of what he normally would be serving the patrons.

Was it the Ridgeway ghost out for entertainment? That's what people say.

Spruce up your ghost tale by adding a rooster

It's no surprise that when a little story or a lengthy spooky legend is told, a few more odds and ends get added to the periphery. The Ridgeway stories are examples of this. It seems like the Welshmen of the area were prone to encounters with the Ridgeway phantom more than the other locals were at odds with the spook. By one account, a Welshman was returning home after a day of working on one of the farms. He had to pass through an area in the pasture that had a stone fence with rails. A mischievous friend dressed in ghost attire sat waiting behind the stone fence for the Welshman. You can imagine what happened next. The bonus here is that the friend had a white rooster, which he was holding on top of his head. This adds a little drama and noise to the fiasco.

As the Welshman climbed through the fence rails, the friend in homemade ghost suit popped up from behind the stones while the frightened rooster broke loose, flapped its wings and flew right into the Welshman's face. The poor man, frightened out of his wits, dropped the pitchfork he had been carrying, and ran like a speeding bullet across the pasture. The friend never clued the Welshman in on what happened that day, and that's how a new tale was born. From that day on, the Welshman was obliged to tell his tale of how he ran face-to-face into the Ridgeway ghost, and how the wings of a great white bird literally pushed him across the pasture to safety.

Coat with a dusting of flour
and stir up frenzy

What's a person to do on a hot summer day for excitement? One young man cooked up a recipe that ended up a bit over-spiced. He decided to give his neighbors a little scare since the ghost tales were running rampant at the time. The young man decided to check out a barrel of flour and cover himself from head to toe in the stuff right around nightfall. He then showed up at the houses of various neighbors and made his presence known by peering around doors and through windows. The plot worked marvelously well, except for the fact that you can't fool all of the people all of the time. Remember that saying in case you ever find yourself in a similar situation.

One seasoned farmer, who was said to be a hero of the Blackhawk War of 1832, decided he wasn't going to let any ghost scare him. He loaded his shotgun and went on the chase after the flour ghost. The earthly ghost ran through a small stand of trees, into a ravine, and through other dense woods as the farmer pursued the flour ghost trying to get a perfect shot. Frightened and extremely exhausted, the ghost hid out in a thick tangle of bushes until the guy with the shotgun *literally* gave up the ghost and went home. Another tale now took root as the brave farmer talked up a storm as to how he had run that darn Ridgeway ghost right out of the country, not just the county. Don't ask me what happened to the guy with the flour suit, but I'd bet he's not into baking much.

The Griffon

Wisconsin is surrounded in three directions by water. Because of this unusual configuration and abundant natural resource, we have an extensive and old maritime history. Part of that history is afloat with ghostly sightings of the ships that met their fate on the treacherous and stormy waters of the Great Lakes. One ship in particular, caught our attention. The ship was called the *Griffon*, named after the mythological monster, the griffin, which was half lion and half eagle. The ship was built in 1679 by Rene-Robert Cavalier Sieur de la Salle, a French explorer, in honor of the governor of New France, Count Frontenac (*Comte de Frontenac*), whose coat-of-arms pictured the griffin.

La Salle planned to establish a fleet of ships operating in the upper Great Lakes to carry mostly furs for shipment to Europe.

The ship weighed 45 tons, was 60 feet long, and was described as "a peculiar ship...full rigged and equipped, having many appointments of a man-of-war." It contained seven cannons and a collection of muskets. It was the first sailing vessel on the Great Lakes that was constructed above Niagara Falls. Metiomek, an Iroquois prophet placed a curse on the ship because it was an offense against the Great Spirit. August 7, 1679 the ship set sail on Lake Erie and headed west towards Green Bay on Lake Michigan.

The ship was then loaded up with beaver pelts in Green Bay, and headed on a return trip east to Niagara where La Salle quickly wanted to pay off his debts with the pelts. He ordered that when the ship arrived in Niagara, it was to return to an area south (Peoria, Illinois) with materials for La Salle to build another ship to explore the Mississippi River. The *Griffon* set sail on September 18 from Detroit Harbor on Washington Island to head back to Niagara. It was never seen again, at least in its usual form.

Without a trace...

What happened to the *Griffon*? La Salle theorized that the crew, headed by the pilot, "Luke the Dane," stole the pelts, sold them and then ridded themselves of the *Griffon*. Some said the Potawatomi or the Ottawa were responsible for the disappearance of the men and the ship. La Salle had heard from the Potawatomi a year later that the ship was spotted in a bay in northern Lake Michigan. Some say the ship met its end in a storm trying to navigate the Door of Death, which refers to the passage between Washington Island and the neighboring islands. Another rumor was that the five crewmembers and pilot Luke the Dane had been observed on the Mississippi with canoes full of pelts, but four of the men met a murderous end along the way. The only survivor, folks surmised, was Luke the Dane who was headed off to trade the pelts.

But where is the ship?

What happened to the ship is as much a mystery as what happened to the crew. The heavily traveled Great Lakes served as a watery destination to many a shipwreck. It's no surprise that through the years, several people claimed discovery of the *Griffon*. Just as many claimed they witnessed the apparition of the ship. Nonetheless, a wreck was discovered in 1955 by Orrie Vail of Tobermory near Russell Island, which is near Lake Huron's Bruce Peninsula. The ship discovered could be dated to the age and description of the *Griffon* by examining the size and shape, and the fact that it had hand-hammered bolts that could have been used on the *Griffon*. In one study, an analysis of a threaded iron bar found with nuts and bolts, revealed that the iron from the bar was made by a process used in France before the 18th century.

Another *Griffon* tale comes from Manitoulin Island on the western end of Lake Huron. The long time residents of the island say that a ship was found on a desolate beach on the western tip of the island, but it was stripped of its iron bolts and lead caulking by settlers on the island. The wood that was left and the design of the vessel were consistent of a ship that would have been made around the time of the *Griffon*.

White rabbit without a pocket watch

William Cullis who was the Mississagi Strait lightkeeper and his assistant John Holdworth, were looking around the shoreline for a tree that would make a good boat spar one day in the late 1800's. Oddly, they happened to stir up a white rabbit that quickly jumped out of sight. Curious about a white rabbit in the wild, John Holdworth went in search of the cottontail. Pulling at brambles, weeds, and undergrowth, John came upon the entrance to a cave. He stepped inside, and to his horror, he was met by a grisly sight—the skeletons of six men. Sometime later, the skulls, kept by local residents, were lost over the years. However, one skull apparently was abnormally large. This would fit with the physical description of the violent Luke the Dane who was reported to be seven feet tall with a huge lumbering frame.

Those who keep a watch for phantom ships have reported seeing the image of the *Griffon* along the north end of Lake Michigan with sails fully set. Many Washington Islanders believe the ship was lost in the Door ("Door of Death" or "*Porte des Morte*"), which, as mentioned earlier, is a treacherous area between Washington Island and the northern tip of the peninsula.

Specter in the glow of yellow moonlight

A story, called the *Vanishing Ship* comes out of an account told in Washington Island history. Late in July on an overcast night, the clouds were sparsely painted by a yellowish tinge of moonlight. The crew of the *Kelly,* a small cruiser, headed towards Gill's Rock as it passed through the Door. The crew planned to reach Gill's Rock before the darkest of night set in, after spending the day in protected waters of Rowley's Bay. But the Door and its turbulence can be deceiving. The open waters of Lake Michigan sprouted three and four-foot waves with gale force winds late that day. The perilous journey took the small boat north along the shore where they rounded Spider Island and passed Gravel Island and Europe Bay. Heading out into open water from North Port dock, they encountered rough whitecaps and unpredictable crosscurrents.

A black outline of Pilot Island and Detroit Island set the stage. One of the women on the boat suddenly spotted an unexpected light. "It's a ship! I can see lights on both ends and along the sides." Her husband in astonishment said the ship was huge. The crew wondered if the ship was the ferry headed for Washington Island, but the hour was late, so this was not likely. As their little boat, the *Kelly*, crested the next wave, the mystery ship passed through the light of the yellow half moon. To their shock, the ship appeared to be an old wooden sailing vessel, with three masts, and full sail. It was the kind of ship, one would see on the Great Lakes in the 1800's or earlier. It headed south towards Gill's Rock. The *Kelly* dipped into the trough of a wave. When it again peaked at the crest of the next wave, the crew found that the large ship had totally vanished. Moments later, the *Kelly* crossed the same path, but there was still no sign of the huge sailing ship at full sail. The crew calls the experience "unforgettable."

Our gratitude for this information goes to the Buffalo and Erie County Historical Society, Washington Island History at Washington Island.com, and the account of Megan Long in her book Ghosts of the Great Lakes.

The Curiosity of Ghost Ships

Nobody can "prove" the existence of ghost ships, just as it is difficult to pin your thumb on the existence of ghosts in general. Again, how can you verify such an event as the sighting of a phantom ship? It could be a mirage or perhaps it is a ship that is so far in the distance that it's hard to make out much detail other than something about it is odd—discordant. Some say an optical illusion of a ship is caused by refraction of light hovering about the horizon, making the ship appear to sail through the sky.

Ghost ships usually seem to be connected to disaster or foreboding times, and they are most likely spotted at the site where the ship was lost. In the lore of superstition, the sighting of a ghost ship foreshadowed a storm. Abandoned ships are sometimes considered ghost ships because of they mystery surrounding them, and occasionally the ghastly finds on board.

For example, the British ship *Johnson*, was sailing off the coast of Chile when it spotted a highly unusual sight. The crew of the *Johnson* found the ship *Marlborough Glasgow* with the masts and sails covered by a mossy growth. Twenty skeletons were found on board in various parts of the ship. The aged ship departed from Littleton, New Zealand in 1890, and disappeared until the *Johnson* discovered it again in 1913. That's 23 years at sea without a trace. "Ghost ship" also refers to every day real ships that are decommissioned for pragmatic reasons. The ships of rich legend, the cream of the crop, however, are the Phantom Ships — the *Griffon*, the *Edmund Fitzgerald*, and many others.

Sailors were at the mercy of the water, the weather, the nature of the crew, and superstition. The figurehead of the ship was said to ward off evil sea serpents and calm the storms. Tattoos came with their own cache of luck. A tattooed crucifix tagged the sailor for a Christian burial if the ship went down and the sailor was later found. A rooster and a pig tattooed on a sailor's knee meant that the sailor would not go hungry by running out of bacon and eggs.

Ravensholme Hille Curse
Waukesha County

The author Stephen King could have written the story of Ravensholme, and we'd all recognize it as "something out of a Stephen King novel." It's truly that gruesome. This is the story of a farmhouse, its people, and its land, said by many to be cursed, and said by some to be haunted at the very least. I was particularly interested in writing about this since I grew up in the lake country of Waukesha County, which is one hop west of Milwaukee County. Not that this is a significant detail, but I can vouch for this part of Wisconsin being rather fraught with pockets of paranormal activity, or what might seem to be paranormal.

Wisconsin was admitted to the Union in 1848, which is when this story begins. John Hille, age 37 settled with his wife Magdelena and their children on 146 acres of untouched wilderness with the intent of going into the farming business. Hille was born in Hanover, Germany and immigrated to the United States in 1837 along with his stern German propensity to get the work done. He was 26 years old at the time, and both of his parents were deceased. John learned the trade of cabinetry in his native Germany and put his skills to work in New York. Life changed for John Hille in 1837 when he married Magdelena, also an immigrant. The couple headed west to a frontier in Wisconsin where there was a high concentration of German immigrants. Supposedly, many of them settled in this area because the green hilly landscape reminded them of their homeland.

Life was good in the log cabin that John built. The farm grew and prospered to 215 acres, and eventually the land was home to granaries, barns, and most notably, a large stone farmhouse. When John cleared his fields, he had salvaged the granite boulders, which were abundant in this Kettle Moraine area of the state. According to belief, the first victim of the curse was Magdelena Hille in 1898, although, by 1880 two of the children had died. Michael died in childhood and John, Jr. died at age 30. The story about Magdelena says that she had been ill, a doctor was summoned, and he accidentally gave her an overdose of "poison." What really happened is unknown. However, in thumbing through *Merck's 1899 Manual of the Materia Medica*, I see there were several compounds that we might think twice about today. These include compounds containing arsenic for diabetes, curare given "hypodermically" with "caution: avoid getting this into a wound, as this may prove fatal," ergot for "hypodermatic use," and cyanide for "tubercular affections" and lupus. Maybe the cure was worse than the disease, as the saying goes.

John Hille lived to age 90 and died of natural causes. With the death of an invalid son shortly after John, sons Oscar and William, along with a sister named Hulda, inherited the entire estate. The other siblings had moved to other parts of the country and had no desire to farm. Adult children escaping the farming life of Wisconsin is a common phenomenon. Nonetheless, the farm continued to thrive very well under the diligence and hard work of the family, and they were respected, trusted, and liked by neighbors.

It's said that the curse continued with the death of Oscar in 1916. He was tethering a bull to post in its stall, when the animal quite unexpectedly lunged at Oscar, causing extensive and fatal internal injuries. Death by bull may seem unusual; however, it is not unheard of, as those in the business will tell you. Perhaps this was all a precursor to what evil was yet to come to the homestead two years later.

By now, World War I was raging in Europe. The remaining siblings, William and Hulda, of German heritage with German customs, were feeling ill at ease. William, in particular would not discuss the war. "It's useless to argue," he'd say. People speculate that neighbors may have been suspicious of William and Hulda's allegiance. Family members strongly discounted this notion.

As trusting as they were, William and Hulda were persuaded by Elder Krause, claiming to be from South Milwaukee, to hire him for farm work. Days later, Krause informed William and Hulda that he was an agent of the Secret Service and he was planted on the farm to ascertain their loyalty to the United States. Of course, Krause was a con man with a bend toward extorting money from the farmers. A neighbor boy, Ernest Fentz, was summoned by Krause to help with odd jobs around the farm. The boy's true job was to help Krause blackmail William and Hulda, and convince the two that Krause and Fentz would expose them as Americans loyal to the enemy in Europe.

The reality is that William and Hulda gave generously to patriotic American causes, including the war in Europe. Prior to Krause hatching his blackmail scheme, William had always liked the young Ernest Fentz. Indeed, he had given him gifts and invited him to take a ride in the newly purchased, new fangled automobile. But when Ernest came under Krause's evil influence and blackmail plan, William fired the boy in late June and told him never to return to the Hille farm.

July 11, 1918. A sinister sequence of events forever marked this day in the history of the Hille farm. Krause picked up the young Ernest Fentz at the Fentz home early in the morning saying that he had a job for him to do. Ernest's stepfather tried to convince the boy not to go with Krause, but Ernest would not listen. After arriving at the Hille farm, Krause and Fentz talked William Hille out of $30, a large sum of money in those days, to "keep quiet" about his anti-American activities, and protect William from certain "exposure." Hulda Hille, who was convinced that Krause and Fentz were out to harm her and her brother William, called the neighbor Mrs. William Dingeldine, and asked the neighbor to hurry to the Hille house. As Mrs. Dingeldine entered the house, a blast resonated from the living room. William then walked into the kitchen carrying a shotgun. He offered to shake hands with Mrs. Dingeldine, but the woman attempted to grab the gun.

Hulda stepped in and said, "No, let him go. It's for the best." She said to Mrs. Dingeldine that she and William would be dead before the authorities would arrive. Ernest Fentz, with the left side of his face no longer attached to his head, was lying dead slumped over the rocking chair in the living room. William walked swiftly toward the barn, convinced that "they were after him." He would not listen to reason as Mrs. Dingeldine pleaded with him. Hulda handed her neighbor a wooden box and begged her to leave, taking the box, which contained valuable papers that she feared Krause, would get a hold of. Mrs. Dingeldine ran towards the road to seek help from neighbors. Reaching the gate, she heard the sound of shotgun blasts coming from the barn. Then she heard Hulda yelling at Krause to stay away. Krause took off running across a field.

The barn was dripping in blood. William, one by one, had shot his five horses. He then walked back to the kitchen and shot the dog. Hulda lie dying upstairs next to an empty bottle of arsenic. She had slit her wrists. The house was quiet. One last blast came from William's bedroom, as he sat in his chair, holding the shotgun between his legs and balancing it against his torso. A strip of wood became the deadly instrument used to push the trigger of the gun.

By the afternoon of July 11, 1918, there were three dead people and six dead animals on the Hille farm. Why? Because the entities known as "They" were after William. The recipe for an extortion plot gone awry included two paranoid elderly people, a rather stupid wanna-make-a-dishonest-buck guy, and a naive young farm hand who came along for the ride. Season this recipe with suspicion of collusion with the German enemy and add a dash of emotional turmoil. Marinade for a bit, and then see what happens.

A coroner's inquest that included gathering information from the three remaining sisters, proved to be of little help in providing answers to this tragedy. Krause was caught in St. Paul, Minnesota, trying to enlist in the Army. He supposedly was brought back to Waukesha by the authorities, but the coroner's report did not include any statement from Krause.

Just when you think this is straightforward horror, another twist weasels its way into the story. Think back to the wooden box that Hulda gave to Mrs. Dingeldine. There was a letter in the box. It read, "Say girls, there was a slapping noise on the wall. I knew what that meant, so good-bye. All be good with Eliza. There are only these three left. We will try our best to get our rights. Don't take it hard, because Bill would have gone to prison for life; he [Krause] was telling Bill about the Japs [sic] coming over and how they will come. And then Bill—we would go in the house and shoot them. Give the machine [car?] to H. and A. That is W's wish." The opposite side of the letter paper listed the pallbearers that Hulda wanted at her funeral.

Some say the curse of Hille farm started the diabolical cascade of dominos that resulted in the slaughter that hot summer day, and continued to move through time. The farm was turned over to one of the sisters, Mrs. Jacob Hahn of Delafield, and she sold it in 1918 to H.S. Kuhtz. The farm reverted to Mrs. Hahn in 1927 after Kuhtz built a milkhouse, enlarged the barn, and went bankrupt. In 1927, a young couple lived in the house for two years, but moved when their two children died of a mysterious "crib death." The house stood empty for the next twenty years. Unfortunately, misfortune continued to associate with the property. In 1932, Mr. Pratt died while dynamiting stone in one of the pastures.

September 1948. Mr. and Mrs. Ralph Ransome, owners

of health spas in Chicago were driving in the area looking for property that they might use as a place to retire to someday, outside of the busy city life. The deserted stone house, with its thirteen beautiful oak trees, still belonged to Mrs. Hahn, the only surviving sister from the Hille family. She agreed to sell the house to the Ransome couple if they agreed to restore the house to its original magnificence. The expensive restoration took four years to complete. The roof was removed, and the interior of the house was rebuilt preserving the 18-inch thick granite stone exterior walls. No expense was too great. The stained glass windows came from a funeral home, a marble fireplace from a New Orleans mansion, and crystal chandeliers came from the McCormick mansion in Chicago.

Neighbors warned the Ransomes, and their married daughter Anita Kennedy, about the curse that would befall anyone who lived in the house—tear it down, dynamite it, don't live in it. In 1953, Anita and her husband moved into the house. In 1963, their seven-year-old son drowned in Lake Mendota in Madison. But after that, the Hille curse remained dormant until nine years later when it struck with a vengeance. By this time, the farm estate was called Ravensholme, after the original English spelling of the Ransome last name. It was 1971 and Ralph and Dorothy Ransome were now retired and living at the house with their five-year-old grandson, Ransome Kenney. Disaster and heartbreak struck on March 17, 1972, when the child was playing in the barn. He fell onto an auger, and the lethal curse claimed another victim.

Summer, 1972. Dorothy Ransome often sat at her kitchen table reading, or stringing beans. She began seeing the figure of a man, or the shadow of a man, moving towards the kitchen door, but when she moved to open the door, nobody was there. She said she thought it was just a shadow, but the sightings of the ghost either near the kitchen door or in the driveway, have occurred on several occasions.

Dorothy believed it was the ghost of John Hille, the original owner of the farm. He wore a black coat and an old hat. The ghost was swinging his arms, and walking fast, usually toward the kitchen door, only appearing in the daytime. The cat of the house often sat up and stared at the kitchen door at the same time the apparition was present. Dorothy theorized that John Hille put so much of his life into building the farm and clearing the land, and just living and loving it all, that he remains there today. She said she is not fearful of the ghost. The neighbors, on the other hand, are as afraid of the place and its alleged curse today as they've always been. The Ransome family laughed at the notion of a curse, and didn't believe in the hogwash at first. "But there has been a constant stream of tragedies right straight through. It's always been the same," said Dorothy.

Cursed? Maybe. Haunted? It's hard to say. The repeated sightings of an apparition are a clue. Serious and some-times fatal farm accidents are common, but the torture of paranoia and its consequences are not included in what we think of as farm accidents. Cursed? Reader is the judge on this one.

(Informational source: Haunted Wisconsin *by Michael Norman and Beth Scott. Trails Books, 2001, and* Haunted Wisconsin *Heartland Press, 1980.* Merck's 1899 Manual of Materia Medica, *Ghosts of the Prairie website)*

Summerwind Mansion
West Bay Lake, Vilas County

Some people would say this is the most haunted house in Wisconsin. Others say, legends of Summerwind are products of the imagination. Those who live in the area are reluctant to give an opinion. The structure burned to the ground in

June 1988 after being hit by lightening in a fierce electrical storm. What remain today are the chimney, the foundation, and the dark tales. Owner, Robert Lamont, lived in Washington D.C., and later served in the Cabinet as Secretary of Commerce for President Herbert Hoover. He built the house in 1916 as a summer retreat.

An indication of something awry in the house was evidenced by two bullet holes that were fired into the basement door by Robert Lamont. Legend has it that he was shooting at a ghost. After Lamont died, the house was sold more than once, and nothing unusual was reported except for the shooting incident. Then in the early 1970's

Arnold and Ginger Hinshaw and their six children moved into Summerwind. They were only able to tolerate the house for six months. The entire family reported ill-defined shapes and shadows present in the hallways. Whispering voices mumbled in dark and empty rooms, but the sounds would stop when a family member entered the room. The ghost of a woman was often seen by the doors that lead to the dinning room.

Appliances would periodically be in need of repair, but would mysteriously begin working again before anyone could call a service man. Windows and doors had a mind of their own, and would open and close without human assistance. Out of exasperation, Arnold Hinshaw nailed one very bothersome window shut, and this seemed to cure the problem. This was minor when compared to Arnold's car that burst into flames. No one was injured or near the car, but the cause of the fire remains a mystery.

When the family decided to make some renovations to the house, they ran into difficulty hiring people to do the renovations. Some of the workers just outright informed the family that the house had a reputation of being haunted, and the workers didn't want to have anything to do with it. One of the tales tells us of a bedroom closet that had a shoe storage drawer in the back wall of the closet. When Hinshaw pulled

out the drawer to paint the frame, he noticed a deep space
behind the drawer. He took a flashlight and peered into the
space. Something was jammed into the narrow spot. But
what? Thinking it was probably an animal that had been
trapped there years ago; he waited until his daughter Mary
came home from school so she could help him determine
what was in the space.

Mary, with flashlight in hand, crawled back into the narrow opening. A scream filled the room. A human skull with
black hair, the skeleton of an arm and part of a leg frightened
the girl. It has been said that the authorities were never contacted, and the reason behind this is unknown. Was there
really a body to begin with, or was this a tale embellished
through the years? The skeleton may not have been disturbed,
but things started happening around the house that hadn't
happened before.

You have to wonder if this isn't something out of Stephen
King's *The Shinning*, but according to the story, Arnold
Hinshaw became quite the organist. He stayed up late at
night to play the organ, but his usual relaxing music turned
to a concoction of unrelated notes and ominous melodies.
The incessant playing continued into all hours of the night,
growing steadily louder. Hinshaw believed demons were
directing his music. He had a mental breakdown and ended
up hospitalized. Ginger, his wife attempted suicide around
the same time.

It appears as though Arnold Hinshaw had not made a good
recovery, and eventually Ginger and the children moved to
Granton, Wisconsin in Clark County to live with Ginger's
parents. A few years later, Ginger's father, Raymond Bober
decided to buy Summerwind and turn it into a restaurant
inn. He was a popcorn vender and businessman, and was
sure he could make a go of a new business. Bober knew
nothing about Ginger's experiences with the paranormal
at Summerwind. She was horrified at the prospect of her
parents dealing with this house, and she urged them not to

buy the property.

Not wanting to hear any of this, Bober announced that he knew the house was haunted by an eighteenth century explorer named Jonathan Carver who was still hunting for an old deed. Reportedly, the document came from the Sioux Indians and granted Carver the upper one-third of Wisconsin. Bober said the ghost indicated the deed was sealed into the foundation of the house, and the ghost wanted help finding this long lost deed. In 1979, Bober wrote a book titled *The Carver Effect*. The book chronicled Bober's communication with the ghost through dreams, trances, and the Ouija board.

After the purchase of the house, Bober, his son Karl, and Ginger along with her new husband George went to inspect the place. George found the closet on the second floor where the shoe drawer hid the secret compartment. As he pulled out the drawer, Ginger frantically begged him to stop. George knew nothing about the prospect of a body buried in the space behind the drawer. Ginger told her story to the group, and moments later, her brother Karl was peering into the blackness of the space with a flashlight. What he found might surprise you. He crawled out of the space and declared it empty. George and Bober also looked in the space and found nothing. Was there ever a body to begin with? Why was there even a clandestine compartment?

Karl traveled to the house later that summer to work on the house and to inquire with someone about getting rid of the bats. He was in the house when it started to rain. As Karl closed windows on the second floor, he heard a voice call his name. No one was around. Karl then went downstairs, walked into the front room and heard two pistol shots. He ran toward the sound in the kitchen and found a smoky room and the smell of gunpowder. He looked at the two bullet holes in the kitchen door to the basement and easily determined that the holes had been there a long time. Was this a timeless tape replaying itself for Karl? He didn't wait to find out. Karl left the house rather quickly.

Turning the house into a restaurant was not to be. Workers complained of tools disappearing, and soon could not tolerate the eerie atmosphere. Bober thought the greatest mystery was the seemingly impossible shrinkage and expansion of the house.

He would measure the room one day, and the next day, he'd find that the measurements had changed notably. When comparing them to the blueprints of the house, Bober found the rooms were substantially larger than indicated on the blueprints. Incredibly, he'd estimate his restaurant could seat 150 people, and then the next day the blueprint would show only enough room for 75 people.

Photographs taken seconds apart with the same camera showed obvious differences in area, especially in the living room. Bober compared his photos of the living room with the photos his daughter, Ginger, and her husband Arnold, had taken when they lived there. Remarkably, the group discovered that the living room curtains Ginger had taken with her when she and Arnold moved out were now back in the photo, only this time on Bober's photos!

It was as if time was repeating itself, just as with Bober's son Karl's experience with the gunshots. Is the explanation simply that Summerwind is a place where time and physics take on qualities that we have yet to understand? If that were the case, perhaps then Summerwind is not haunted at all, but the shadows and figures are trapped in time and reappear according to...according to what? Some things remain beyond our comprehension, but that does not exclude them from happening.

Oddly enough, the Bobers never spent a night in the house, and the place never became a restaurant or an inn. Raymond Bober decided that the ghost of Jonathan Carver was too restless to let any mortal renovate the house until his lost deed was found. The deed, supposedly buried in the foundation, has never been found.

Summerwind Gone with the Wind

After years of rumors, tales and speculation about Summerwind, a variety of skeptics have analyzed the claims of Raymond Bober. But their claims are sometimes as bizarre as the original claims of haunting. Summerwind is now gone with the wind. What remains are the witness accounts, the reports from the Bober family, and the musings of those who bypass the unexplainable. Will Pooley, a freelance writer, worked to research and gather facts in 1983 on Summerwind in hopes of discrediting the fantasia. Pooley said that even if Bober had found Carver's deed, it would have been worthless because the British government prohibited the purchase of Indian land. In addition, he claimed the Sioux never claimed land in that large area, thus it was not theirs to give.

The argument says that the land was given to Carver; he did not purchase it, thus British law would not apply. Furthermore, the Sioux represented a nation, not a single tribe, and it is very likely that one tribe of the Sioux nation could have lived in Wisconsin. Pooley said the deed to the property had been located in the land office in Wausau, Wisconsin in the 1930's, and he speculated that it was unlikely Carver traveled to the far north West Bay Lake. The question arises, would he actually have had to travel to West Bay Lake to hold a deed to it? Maybe Poole's most convincing argument is that the deed could not have been placed in the foundation, because Summerwind was built 130 years after the death of Jonathan Carver, and the contractor who poured the foundation of the house in 1916 stated that nothing had been placed in the foundation.

Did Bober ever actually own the land called Summerwind? Local residents say he spent less than two summers on the property, abandoned his plan to establish a restaurant and inn, considered opening a concession stand, and had plans to conduct haunted house tours. But did he really own the land? One resident said Bober tried to buy the house, but the deal fell through, and accordingly the house was abandoned for unknown reasons.

Summerwind Epilogue

Was the house really haunted, as Bober claimed, or was this a convenient way to lure a crowd to the fantasy of a haunted restaurant? Many of the doubting questions come from neighbors annoyed with the intrusion of tourists who came by busload to go on a ghost hunt. The ravages of time in the 1980's pushed the house deeper into ruin where bats now had set up a large condominium village. In 1986, three investors bought the place complete with its shattered windows and open doors, but in June 1988, lightning started a fire and Summerwind burned. What's left today of the mysterious mansion are chapters etched in time—stone chimneys, the deedless foundation, and its murky unknown, and perhaps paranormal, history.

Part of this account is based on "Summerwind, Wisconsin's Most Haunted House," an article for Ghosts of the Prairie Magazine *and website by Troy Taylor. Several resources exist on Summerwind.*

Has the curse finally calmed down?

T.B. Scott Mansion, Merrill, Wisconsin

A mansion with a curse is nothing new. The T.B. Scott Mansion in Merrill, Wisconsin pops up every so often if you're looking into Wisconsin ghost stories. However, there doesn't really seem to be any haunting activity, just one of those every day curses declared by an Indian chieftain of the village called Squitee-cau-sippi. The chief's beautiful daughter, named Jenny by the settlers, was rumored either to have killed herself because of her love for a young lumberjack, or to have died of influenza. Jenny's father wished her buried on the hill across the river from the settlement. On the day of her burial, he cursed the land saying that no white man should ever benefit from it. The land became known as "Jenny's Hill" or "Jenny Bull Falls."

I guess those words started things rolling. The Native American settlement was abandoned after a number of years and the area was taken over by T. B. Scott who was a wealthy lumberman and mill owner. He purchased this piece of land in 1886 from the government with the intention of building a grand mansion. Construction began, but two years following the purchase of the land, Scott died, without completing the building of his mansion. The widow, Ann, attempted to complete what her husband had started, but the woman was in very ill health, and she died within the year. The house passed down to Walter, the son of T.B. and Ann. So he tried to complete the project. No luck, Walter died of a letter opener attack from the architect in Chicago who was supposed to work on the place.

Three down...

That's three down with several more to go. Next up is Mr. Kuechle who decided to acquire the estate and use it as a summer retreat from his busy life in Chicago. He bought elaborate furnishings for the house, including hand carved doors, a carved mantel, and embossed mirrors. Apparently, Kuechle never lived in the house. Instead, a turn of bad luck prompted him to mortgage the house to Mr. Barsanti, a tavern owner from Chicago. Other bad investments cropped up for Kuechle, such as using a large sum of money to build a stretch of the Northern Pacific Railroad. This did not work for him, and he died in a mental institution. Barsanti, on the other hand, never lived to see the mansion either. He ran into a snag when he crossed paths with a violent gang in Chicago called the Black Hand. Barsanti was waiting in Chicago's Union Station when one of the gang members stabbed him to death. Ironically, Basanti was on his way to the mansion in Merrill. We're at four deaths now and still counting. His family sold the property along with its uncompleted mansion to a real estate speculator, George Gibson.

Gibson decided to make the place into a home for elderly lawyers. He established an office in Merrill and collected donations to re-establish work on the uncompleted mansion. One late afternoon, he was leaving the office headed towards home to have dinner with his family. Gibson never made it home that day. He simply disappeared. It was quite the mystery. Search parties were organized and the river was dragged, but the odd disappearance was never solved.

All right, now our house has claimed number six, and we're still counting. After Gibson vanished into nowhere, the Barsanti family again took over the house since all the payments had not yet been made by the now invisible Gibson. During the time of ownership by the Barsanti family, the house was never occupied. This continued for many years as the house's sinister reputation grew like a grapevine.

Popcorn Dan rides the Titanic

Groundskeepers maintained the unoccupied property over the years when the Barsanti family owned the place. An old groundskeeper, called Popcorn Dan, because he operated a popcorn stand in Merrill, decided to visit England, where he was born. He set sail in the year 1911. Unfortunately, he returned in 1912 on the *S.S. Titanic.* We can guess how that event concluded. We're now at seven down. After Popcorn Dan came Mr. Lloydson as caretaker. He soon died of alcoholism. Eight down. Next was Mary Fehlhaber, a midwife. She became suddenly ill one day and died at a neighbor's farmhouse before medical help could reach her. Total count is nine. Henry Fehlhaber, husband of Mary, gave the property to the city of Merrill in 1919. In 1923, the city gave the mansion to the Sisters of Mercy of the Holy Cross, who are Roman Catholic nuns.

To this day, the Scott Mansion is used by the nuns as a

The T.B. Scott Mansion in Merrill supposedly was the target of a native chief's curse. (Photo by Brian Borton)

residence. They also operate a hospital and college. Maybe the curse ran out of steam in 1923. No unusual events or deaths have been reported pertaining to the place from 1923 to the present. However, the current residents do not comment on the Scott Mansion or discuss the alleged curse. Does it really continue?

Marie Still Lives on National Avenue
Milwaukee

Marie had been an attractive young woman, and the story goes that she either committed suicide or just mysteriously disappeared. She is said to haunt an old two-story brick house on the 1600 block of National Avenue, Milwaukee. In the late 1970's two men, Paul Ranieri and Jeff Hicks decided to renovate the rundown place. The house had been built sometime between 1836 and 1840 and was still on its original foundation. It had been a private home, an inn, a restaurant, and a rooming house. When the two renovators bought the place, it was unoccupied and neglected. The house was on the demolition list, but the men wanted to preserve the history and the architecture.

Marie was usually an unseen entity, but her presence was detected by the sudden and remarkable coldness in the room. The renovators tolerated her occasional visit. The house was in no shape to live in yet, but a rear apartment at the back of the house was suitable and in good condition to rent out. The first tenant was Donald Erbs, and he actually "met" Marie. Donald said he didn't see a woman enter the room, but "all at once she was there." He said that he thought the woman had been on some business in the house and had wandered to the second floor living room of his apartment. Don asked her questions, but the woman did not respond. She simply stared at him with a face that "seemed out of sync with the rest of the room." The woman had this strange glow about her. "It was as if somebody had a spotlight on her, and she was overexposed and brighter than the surroundings." It was difficult to describe.

Marie was barefoot and wore an ankle-length nightgown with lace. She had long brown hair. What's quite surprising is that the ghost began to talk about the house, according to Don. She talked about the person who built the house, when sections of the house were built, and the reason behind remodeling certain areas. After discussing the house, Marie walked out of the room. Don followed a few seconds later, but the woman had disappeared. He contends that it would have been impossible for her physically to leave so quickly. Marie had appeared as a solid form, and it was difficult to say she was a ghost, but Don said that she clearly was not of this world. He talked to Paul Ranieri, one of the owners, about Marie. Paul stated that nobody had been granted permission to be on the property, and he knew of no one who matched the description of the woman.

She saved the potted plant

The next Saturday, Don and the owners were stripping yellowed wallpaper and preparing the hardwood floors for refinishing. Earlier in the morning, Don constructed a shelving unit that he brought from another apartment. When that job was completed, he walked to the main part of the house to work with Paul and Jeff. Suddenly, a crash came from the room where Don had been working on the shelf. Now the shelf was on the floor, but a plant that Don put on the shelf was sitting intact on the floor a few feet away. Apparently, the plant had been moved by unseen forces. Later that evening Don was watching TV when Marie appeared in a chair next to him. He was not quite as startled this time, and asked her about the shelf. She replied that she had bumped into it accidentally, but saved the plant. Marie assured Don that she meant no harm, and that she was pleased the house was being renovated. And in fact, she would offer the help of her father's carpentry skills. Then the woman suddenly got up and left with no sound of footsteps or closing doors.

Paul Ranieri saw Marie in September, although he did not see her as a solid figure. He had been working on one of the rooms, and said he had the distinct impression that he was being watched. He glanced over to the front hallway staircase and saw the woman glide through an archway and melt into the wall. She did not speak. The woman fit Don's description, except that Paul could see the wall and furniture through the woman.

About ten days later, Don again encountered Marie, however this time she was transparent and standing near the bedroom door. He was startled, and the figure quickly vanished. Weeks later, Marie was again in Don's apartment. Paul and Jeff had begun work on the basement that was originally sectioned off into small, damp cubicles. The basement was littered with broken dishes, jars, and old furniture. They suspended the work until they could contact an urban archeologist at a university to examine the articles. Marie called on Don again. She wondered why the basement work had stopped.

Don tried to explain, but Marie led him to a wall in the basement, pointed to it, and then disappeared. Don contacted Paul and Jeff. The next day they examined the wall, found it to be newer than other parts, and decided to dig into the wall crawl space. They found jewelry, pieces of pottery and the bones of a dog who had been buried there.

The men surmised that the recovery of the dog skeleton bones might explain another paranormal event that happened earlier in the renovation. Paul was lying in bed reading one night when he noticed his cat was cowering under the chair. Paul reached over to calm the cat and came face-to-face with a bull terrier. The only real life dog in the house was a Siberian husky downstairs. Jeff had an experience with the ghost dog too. He had been working late one evening in the basement, and heard what sounded like metal dog tags clinking. Jeff turned around expecting to see the husky, but nothing was there, and the door going upstairs remained shut.

The basement lights were troublesome. Paul and Jeff would find the lights in the basement illuminated several times a week. No one had been downstairs to turn the lights on. Three separate switches would have to be turned flipped to light all the bulbs, and the lights could only be turned on from the basement itself.

Gerry and the Hitchhiker

Gerry, a retired trucking company executive, lives a few blocks away from the brick house on National Avenue. He drove by the large house every day, not thinking twice about it. But on a late September night, a few years before his retirement, he was driving down National Avenue in the sixteen-hundred block, and he spotted a young woman in the street trying to catch the attention of passing traffic. It was around 9:00 P.M. on Friday, and Gerry was on his way to watch a bowling team the company sponsored after work. At around 1:00 or 2:00 A.M, he left the all-night restaurant where he stopped after the bowling outing. While he was driving, he spotted a woman who seemed to be in some sort of trouble. Gerry stopped directly in front of the house that Paul and Jeff had remodeled. Without a word, the young woman jumped into the van and pointed down the street.

The woman was in her early twenties and had dark shoulder-length hair. She wore a jacket, slacks, and a blouse. Gerry thought it odd that she did not carry a purse or any other sort of bag. He wondered what she was doing out late at night without identification. Gerry asked the woman where she wanted to go. The woman did not speak, but appeared to make a sort of grunting noise as she pointed down National Avenue, the same way he was headed. Gerry asked her to write her name, and write down the destination. The woman wrote "Mary." She seemed agitated and confused. Gerry continued to drive National Avenue toward 26th Street. The woman frantically motioned for him to turn the corner. They finally ended up on Mineral Street. It was a very dark street, with little illumination from streetlights. There appeared to be no activity in this residential section. A few cars were parked on the street. Gerry said the woman murmured something that sounded like "You nice man."

The mysterious woman opened the door of the van and climbed out. She did not shut the door completely, and the dome light was on. Gerry waited for her to close the door all the way. He thought she might have possibly fallen when the door remained open. Gerry looked out the passenger side window, but saw nothing. He got out of the van, and walked around to the passenger side. Nobody was in sight. Gerry thought this was impossible. It appeared as if the woman simply vanished. He then drove around a little to see if he could again find the troubled young woman. Nothing was in sight but the darkness of night.

When he arrived home, Gerry told his wife Audrey what

had happened. He was starting to think that he had picked up a ghostly hitchhiker, as Audrey remarked about the shocked look, which he brought home with him. However, Audrey was not skeptical. She had heard of such things happening. The couple lives near 38th and Greenfield, and had never taken notice of tales about Marie or the haunting prior to this incident. No other odd encounters happened to Gerry, and he put that strange night nearly out of mind.

About a year later, Audrey gave Gerry an early edition of the book *Haunted Wisconsin* for a Father's Day gift. She wrote the inscription, "For My Own Ghost Hunter." Gerry discovered the story of Marie and pointed it out to Audrey. The early edition of *Haunted Wisconsin* had a picture of the window of the house and they recognized it as the house on National Avenue where Gerry picked up the hitchhiker.

A photo of a young woman was found in the house when Paul and Jeff were renovating it. The photo is published the early edition of *Haunted Wisconsin*. It might be Marie. Her hairstyle is fashionable of one from the 1920's or 1930's. Gerry can't be sure she's the woman he encountered on the night in September. He thinks she had longer hair, but can't be sure. He does know that the destination the hitchhiker wanted to go made no sense. It was a quiet, dark residential area with few lights lit at that time of night.

Gerry is still puzzled." I wasn't frightened, but I just can't imagine where she went that evening or what happened to her. She disappeared so fast."

Gerry tells the story, and people kid him about it, but he firmly believes in the possibility that he gave a ride to a ghost. He'll always wonder.

Information for this story comes from Haunted Wisconsin *(2001) and* Haunted Wisconsin *(1980) by Michael Norman and Beth Scott.*

Ghosts of Marquette University

Marquette University in downtown Milwaukee has a very rich heritage; however, conversations about Marquette usually do not hit on the topic of the school's supply of ghostly inhabitants. Six tales circulate from time to time. The **Helfaer Theater** or the Marquette Theater is allegedly haunted by a former artistic director who died in Studio 13. He is known to bang around on the catwalks, and is observed in the Studio.

Humphrey Hall (Apartments) was a student dormitory for juniors and seniors. This structure was the former Milwaukee Children's Hospital. The morgue was in the basement. It's said that several spirits of the children still haunt the place. Public safety officers report seeing children on camera monitors. Students who live in the dorm report hearing singing, laughing, crying, and screaming, as well as seeing apparitions.

Johnston Hall was the first building erected on campus. Rumor is that a Jesuit priest threw himself off the top floor or the roof, and the spirit still haunts the building. People get strange feelings when they walk down the hall alone. Some reports say two priests threw themselves off the building.

Masuda Hall is one of the dorms where a girl supposedly committed suicide in one of the rooms. Residents who lived in the room since that time report poltergeist activity such as flying objects, writing on fogged windows, and sounds. It's been said that a priest blessed the room, performed something similar to an exorcism, and the activity stopped, and does not continue to this day.

Straz Hall is formerly East Hall, and a YMCA. The rumor is a little boy named Petey drowned in the pool, his ghost still haunts the basement, and you can hear him walk towards you.

Varsity Theater is where a stagehand was apparently smoking a cigarette while on a break. He accidentally leaned into a huge metal fan, which killed him by cutting him to pieces. Whether this ghost is intact or not, we don't know.

Child's Play at Whispering Oaks Restaurant

Bristol (Kenosha County)

Whispering Oak's new owner, Craig Hartung and his father decided to renovate the restaurant in Bristol approximately a decade ago. Strange occurrences began to happen along with the usual disruption of building and fixing. Craig asked his friends to help him remodel the place, so a number of them drove over to the restaurant one day. One friend jumped out of the car, looked at the building, and said, "It's haunted; I'm not going in there." Well, that started the cascade things.

The restaurant staff experienced many odd occurrences over the years. One of the most common, and probably unusual, is what happens when young children come into the restaurant with their parents. The kids ask if they can play with the child "over there." When the parents look, they see nobody. An employee who has worked at the restaurant for years tells of walking through the kitchen early one morning to take a final look, and make sure all was set up for breakfast. He felt a tugging on the back of his shirt and heard a child's voice say, "Will you play with me?" Nobody was there. Another employee was almost struck when a metal bucket flew forcefully off the shelf near the stereo system. One day the staff heard a loud crash coming from the kitchen. They rushed in to see the heavy special washing bag that was loaded with flatware lying on the floor several feet away from the countertop. The conclusion was that the ghost does not like to be ignored.

Craig, the owner, said he didn't pay much attention to the paranormal events, until one morning when things became a little more dramatic. The restaurant staff was sitting at a table talking before diving into the day's hectic lunch hour preparations. They began to hear strange noises in the kitchen—tings, as if a pan connected with a hard surface. The noise was unusual enough that the staff rushed to the kitchen to see exactly what was happening. To everyone's amazement, all of the sauté pans had been taken from their hooks and arranged into a perfect fan shape on the floor.

The wine also became problematic. "In all the years we've owned this restaurant, we've never, never, ever had trouble with the wine," said owner Craig. He had been walking through the restaurant's storage area when three bottles popped their corks one after another. The last cork almost hit Craig in the shoulder, which was a distance of seven or eight feet. "One bottle might go because of changing atmospheric conditions, but two is unusual, and three is unheard of." The third cork flew the distance, and was from a nonsparkling vintage. The wine should not have had the rocket fuel required to throw a cork that far.

Playful ghosts are creative it seems. Another time Craig and several employees heard a musical ring of glass. They followed the sound into the barroom, and found a single shot glass taken from the middle of a pyramid of glasses and placed exactly in the ray of the only beam of sunlight coming through the window.

(Information from the Burlington News, *Janet Deaver, and Spirit of Geneva Lakes)*

Tales of Nashotah House
Delafield, Wisconsin

Nashotah House, home to an Episcopal seminary, was founded in 1842, and started with three students. The establishment was chartered in 1847, making it the oldest chartered institution of higher learning in Wisconsin. The beautiful area is neatly tucked away off Highway C north of

Delafield. You can't see it from the road. I remember playing there a few times as a child, and being a tree climber, I was always impressed by the very large trees on the grounds.

A common tale heard about Nashotah house says the area has been inhabited since around the 1500's. It's said that in the mid to late 1700's a seminary student was hanged allegedly by his wife who was having an affair with the dean of the seminary. The murder was to appear as a suicide, however, on her deathbed the guilt-ridden wife confessed to the crime. The young man had been buried in a cornfield to admonish him for the sin of committing suicide. The seminarians then decided to bury the young priest in a cemetery to acknowledge that he had not committed the grievous sin. When they went to exhume the casket, they found it empty. The legend is that the seminarian haunts the grounds to this day. The dates on this are suspicious, perhaps putting this tale more into the folklore realm.

Black Monk

An account coming out of Nashotah House is that of the Black Monk. Daniel Pope was a Roman Catholic monk living at Our Lady of Spring Bank Seminary in nearby Oconomowoc Lake. In 1852, he was found hanged in his cell. Daniel's fellow monks requested that he be buried at Nashotah House, but because suicide was considered a mortal sin, he was denied burial in the seminary's consecrated cemetery, and buried elsewhere on the grounds. As the story goes, twenty years later, a monk confessed to the murder of Daniel Pope, but Nashotah House officials refused to move the body. The ghost, known as the Black Monk, has been roaming the grounds ever since in his black robe seeking his rightful resting place.

News articles over the years have reported a variety of spirits roaming the campus. A *New York Times* article published on December 7, 1902, noted that apparitions were seen on the day Reverend James Lloyd Beck, one of the founders of the seminary was buried in 1876. Another account talks about the spirit of Azel Cole, an early Dean of the school who died in 1886, and still likes to wander the halls. The *Lake Country Reporter*, a local newspaper, published an article in 2002, which noted the daughter of a seminarian reported seeing a ghostly figure wearing a hooded robe walking toward her in a hallway in 1983.

A priest, Tom Papazoglakis, at St. Bartholomew Episcopal Church in Pewaukee, and former seminarian at Nashotah House, says that rather than producing fright, the ghost stories of Nashotah House perhaps reinforce the spirituality and holiness of Nashotah House. "I don't think it's considered haunted in the sense that there's anything to be scared of. It's more like a spiritual presence. They even named a seminary football team the Black Monks."

Hasslinger's Moose Lake Beach
Nashotah, Wisconsin

Hasslinger's was a wild time resort. It was rather hidden down a long winding little country road dotted with summer cottages and tall lush trees along the lake. There were no streetlights for a long time, so when it was dark, it was *very* dark. The best nights were when light of the full moon sparkled on the water. On the drizzly moonless nights, it was truly spooky. I can still hear water from the leaves higher in the trees actually dripping on to the lower leaves when a slight wind whispered.

The place has been overrun now with awkwardly large houses that seem to be too big for their britches, and gobble up the land like sharks in frenzy. But there was a time, not too long ago, when the resort was a central entertainment point, although far enough out of the way, that visitor could escape the city or mundane activities of life. It was an adventure, almost like going to Oz. Originally; the place was called the

Evergreen Resort and was owned by a Mr. Miller. Herbert J. Hasslinger bought the land in 1920 at the age of 23 or 24. He graduated from Marquette University in Economics in 1915, and carried the nickname "Buckshot" amongst his classmates.

World War I caught up with Herbert in 1917, and he was shipped to France as an accountant with the U. S. Army. I remember seeing a letter he had sent to June Rose Clark, his wife-to-be. He was stationed in Texas at the time, and the men on base were dying off from the Spanish flu pandemic that later swept through Europe and other parts of the world, killing around 25 million people. He hoped he could survive that.

The Hasslinger Moose Lake Resort was a drawing place for people from Chicago, including the rather nefarious gangster types, coming up to spend a week or two in the summer. The Illinois visitors would catch the train from Chicago to Nashotah or Oconomowoc. Hasslinger's survived Prohibition, and in fact, operated throughout Prohibition with a little help from local stills on the property and bootlegging operations—after all, Herb was a sharp businessman. He told of the times in the late 1920's and early 1930's when the Chicago mobsters would try to "sell him protection" partly because he had slot machines at the resort, and then there was that small matter of the liquor, which was buried across the road and in the expansive yard.

Herbert and the family ran the resort, dancehall, and a large commercial apple orchard for decades. They had a few cows. People would come from the city to get milk and buy ice, which was cut from the lake in the winter and stored in the icehouse.

The property was home to several structures including a main house that had eight bedrooms. A large dancehall and bar, a boathouse at the lakefront, an icehouse, and a red barn built into the hill so that it could have an upper barn and a lower barn, three sheds, and a pavilion on the lower end of the lake property comprised the buildings. Two summerhouses, one on either end of the property, were the bookends.

Herbert had a small apple orchard on the hill and a large 500-tree apple orchard in the valley mingled with a few pear trees and cherry trees. There was a marsh area appropriately called "the swamp," a baseball diamond with a little "golf shack," and easy-to-get-lost-in woods on the hill above the large orchard. Herbert even tapped two springs in the lake so that we'd always have cold spring water to drink. People from Milwaukee came out to fill jugs full of water until the "authorities" shut down the springs because the water wasn't tested, despite the fact that nobody reported any illness. We'd been drinking it for years.

Family ghosts according to mother...

We never paid a lot of attention to the strange occurrences that went on around the place. It was a hopping place, and we all had plenty to do from April through December of every year. But I do recall my mother saying, "Oh, those are just family ghosts." The explanation seemed good enough at the time and satisfied the inquiring mind initially. And curiously enough, she said that Spiffy, June Rose's stepsister came to the place as a young girl and expected to see ghosts.

It seemed like the eeriest things happened in the dancehall. We think the structure was built around 1938. Doors would slam and windows on hinges would rattle and close. Occasionally a windowpane would break. The men's bathroom door would open and close loudly on its own. It had a very distinct noise of a heavy door that needed a little grease. There was a dark and dusty broom room on one end of dancehall. Many employees were reluctant to go into that cramped little room because of the onset of a sort of sinking anxious feeling. You just wanted to get out quickly. The back end of the dancehall served as a "cloakroom" for people who would come to the Saturday night dances. There was a curious little door in the cloakroom that blended into the texture and color of the wall.

Hartland, Wis.
"Buckshot"   Economics.
   Besides being a business man "Buckshot" knows
all about farming, so with this great store of
knowledge he should leave college well equipped
to take up the business of earning a living. "Buckshot" entered school with the one great quality that
makes a good student—unlimited curiosity. Even
the very exhaustive lectures of the Dean on such
subjects as the wool industry failed to satisfy his
longing to know all about every thing and he was
continually asking questions. For this reason he
has learned all that there is to know on all subjects he has studied and examination days present
little terror for Herbert John.

H. J. Hasslinger.

Herbert J. Hasslinger, pictured here in the entry from
the 1915 Marquette University yearbook, is said to keep
watch over his beloved land.

The alleged haunted dance hall at Hasslinger's Moose
Lake Resort in Waukesha County. (Photo from the Mary
Hasslinger collection)

It was an escape of some sort and seemed to be only accessible from the inside of the building.

We had a dog "Moose" who was half beagle half-German shepherd. Moose had the short legs of a beagle and the body of a German shepherd. He was quite the sight, but a very loyal dog that could race any cat when it came to claiming nine lives. Moose could even walk up the steps of the water-slide with his short legs, and then slide down. Picture it. If Moose were in the back of the dancehall, he would on occasion stare at and bark at the empty stage. This was always rather perplexing. At night, the place brought the sound of creaking boards and sometimes footsteps. Just being alone in the dancehall in the daytime was eerie enough at times, especially on cloudy damp days.

Locked in...

Jack Grimm, grandson of Herbert, was locked in the basement cooler more than one time. The old cooler room had a simple "knife lock" that closed from the outside. Once Herb sent Jack down to the basement cooler to tap a keg of beer. Jack found himself locked in. He wasn't sure how he'd get out, so he just untapped the beer and waited for his grandfather to come down to see what the hold-up was.

Clark "Corky" Grimm, another grandson of Herb's was locked in the front porch in the main house many times. Some supplies for the dancehall were kept on the front porch, and Jack sent Corky over to get some cups one day. Well, Corky didn't return in a timely manner, and Jack thought the kid had taken off to participate in a recreational activity—skipped out—in other words. Jack was annoyed, to put it politely. He headed over to the house to see about getting the cups himself. Jack went into the house, walked toward the front porch and found Corky pounding on the large, heavy carved gray door with the carved doorknob. He was "locked in" but the door was not locked.

A paned glass door was also in front of (lakeside) the gray door. This door had a simple hook and eye arrangement that locked from the outside (hallway side). Several times Corky would go to the front porch to retrieve supplies, and the glass door would "lock itself" from the outside (hallway). Nobody else was in the house when this happened. Finally, it became such a problem with the glass door, ghost or not, that it was removed, and the knob was taken off the heavy gray door. The front porch was originally a parlor with a set of French doors in addition to the other doors. The player piano that was in the front porch eventually ended up at The House on the Rock.

The old main house itself was originally built in the 1890's complete with fruit cellar and poured basement walls that divided off a coal bin. The house was always a lively place—so many people in and out. A creaky staircase led to the upstairs, and beyond that, a very narrow staircase led up to a large attic with no electricity. While upstairs in the house, you'd never feel like you were alone—there always seemed to be a presence no matter what room you were in at the time. Some rooms felt "heavier" than others did. June's room on the first level, the kitchen, and the back porch seemed to be the least bothersome.

One apparition was seen in the place around 1954. The apparition was a woman in a Victorian style long dress that had a deep maroon color to it. She did not have a well-defined face. The apparition turned and faded into the attic door. We were not able to find information about anybody dying in the house, however, Grandma Rose Kriesel, had her Wake in the dinning room of the house. Rose was tall and thin.

There seemed to be a fair amount of activity after Herbert Hasslinger died in January of 1981 at the age of 83 or 84. He did not die in the house, however. Some years later, a boarder-care taker for the property, Arthur, had been staying at the house, and he remarked on the activity:

I used to see Grandpa Herb all the time. Also, the door

that went to the attic had a sturdy sliding lock, and that thing would be open so much of the time, despite how many times I'd lock it again. It became annoying. And the wedding dress—that darn wedding dress in the linen closet—I don't know whose it was, but the top of the box would be off, so I'd put it back on again, only to find it off again a few days later. In one of the bedrooms I slept in, I saw 15-20 ghostly 'people' a couple of times. I don't know what that was all about, but I had the distinct impression that the ghosts were 'high rollers.' Stairs creaking and footsteps were common. When Grandpa Herb died, the clock on the mantel stopped. After that, once a year it started up around January and ran for about twelve hours.

Arthur and the Christmas ornament

Arthur went on to tell about his Christmas ornament experience. He had a particular moose ornament given to him by me. The ghost apparently liked to move the ornament from the tree and place it over another ornament that was situated between the two sides of the French doors that led to the front porch.

No matter what I did, I'd get up in the morning, and there would be that ornament hooked between the two French Doors again! I had trouble with the door and the ghost. In the winter, I'd put plastic sheeting over the door to keep the heat in, but there were times I'd come home, and find that the doors were open and the sheeting was torn down. I'd just put it all back up again. Sometimes, there's no pleasing a ghost.

The glass fireplace doors were another area of consternation. At least three times following Herb's death, the left-hand door shattered. The damper was closed and no fire had been going for months. We could not find an explanation. Arthur believes the doors shattered twice before Herb's death also. Another guest at the house, Lauren, said that the day after Herb died, he walked in from the stairway landing, looked around the living room, turned, and retreated to the stairway.

It seems the barn was not free of spirits either. People who had to go into the barn, felt as if they were being watched. Todd Lynch, who was renting space for his carpentry shop in the upper barn, had problems with the radio station tuning itself to a different channel. When the property was sold, the barn was burned in a controlled fire. From the photos that were taken by Mary Hasslinger at that event, it looks as if a face in the curls of smoke is appearing. Perhaps we can't relate that to haunting activity, but it is an unusual photo nonetheless, and it makes you wonder. Another face in a second photo taken by Mary looks as if it is coming from the lower level of the barn.

The here and now

Some people visited Hasslinger's Resort to party and to "get scared." We don't know about any events out of the ordinary that happened on the property, but the earlier history is vague and incomplete. At least two people drowned at the beach resort. Much of the mystery of the place has been lost to time. The house is gone and the landscape has been sculpted to meet the desires of the new property owners. Whether the ghosts remain or not, is unknown. The property belonged to the Hasslinger family for 75 years. One of the summerhouses was thoughtfully renovated by Herb's granddaughter, Connie. She and her husband Todd Lynch, a contractor, had a goal to keep the mystique of the land and use the building materials that blend in with the landscape.

Is the summerhouse haunted? I asked Connie. She doesn't think so, but every once and awhile a few odd harmless things occur. Ted Holsen, another grandson of Herb's, stayed in the house before it was renovated. The house belonged to his mother Elizabeth Hasslinger Holsen at the time. He reports hearing the unmistakable weird sound of ice cracking one night on the lake as it sometimes does in the winter. Ted

The burning barn at Hasslinger's Resort. A face shows in the upper left corner if you use your imagingation. (Photo by Mary Hasslinger)

got out of bed and looked all over the house, but could not find the source of the noise. It could not have been the lake, because it was the middle of summer. It remains a mystery.

Sincere thanks to Mary Hasslinger, Jack Grimm, Joy Hasslinger Grimm, Arthur Wille, and Ted Holsen for their memoirs. This piece was written by Hannah Heidi Levy, granddaughter of Herbert J. Hasslinger.

Giddings's Boarding House
Milwaukee, Wisconsin

Employees of the local tannery stayed at Mrs. William Giddings's boarding house on Milwaukee's South Side. The house was located at the corner of Allis and Whitcomb Streets in Allen's Addition. The two-story house had gained a calm reputation until it all started…

Saturday, August 8, 1874 9:00 in the morning

Mary Spiegel, age fourteen, was the daughter of a Polish family in the area. She was badly abuse by her father, and was happy to have the job at Mrs. Giddings's boarding house away from the attacks of an enraged parent. Mary was understandably in a high state of anxiety most of the time, but Mrs. Giddings treated her well and was understanding.

Pie making in the kitchen was a routine task until that day in August when the spoons leaped from their container and rocketed in all directions about the room. Mrs. Giddings tried to take it all in stride, but this was pretty bizarre. She continued with her work until a noisy kitchen trap door began rising and falling. Mrs. Giddings told Mary to stand on the door, and Mary obeyed, but the young girl was unable to control the door. Mrs. G. thought that perhaps a jokester had gotten into the cellar, so she decided to check it out. Nobody was there. Climbing up from the cellar and back into the kitchen, the frazzled, but still calm, Mrs. Giddings found that the kitchen had turned into a circus.

Warning: This scene has a lot of visual imagery

Dishes went flying from the china cabinet and crashing to the floor, an oil lamp sailed through the air and shattered on the floor, chairs headed toward the ceiling, with one breaking on the descent. A pie fell from the table as the stove danced, a dish of beans spilled, and eggs flew out of the kitchen pantry. One egg was right on target and hit Mrs. Giddings's posterior. Mrs. Giddings sent Mary to fetch the neighbors Mrs. Mead and Mrs. Rowland, because she didn't know what else to do. But maybe if more people were around this unbelievable activity would come to a halt.

Not a chance. A pail of flowers at the door bounded over the five-and-a-half foot wooden fence and into the next yard as Mrs. Mead and Mrs. Rowlings advanced to the Giddings house. The pail was retrieved but it couldn't sit still, and it flew over the fence again. Mary was terribly frightened.

Another Warning—more visual imagery

Four women and a girl, now forming a circle, sat in the kitchen. Mary started to peel potatoes for dinner. A potato flew out of the pan sitting in her lap, and the knife was jerked from her hand. The potato and the knife hit the mortified Mrs. Rowlings. Then a dish on the table cracked in half, with one half falling to the floor. The corn boiling on the stove decided to get in on the action and leaped out of the pot. The ever-steady Mrs. Giddings tried to remain composed. What, are you kidding? Mrs. Mead politely excused herself like a bat out of hell, and went, no...flew home.

The terrified Mrs. Mead had just reached her yard when a heavy wooden stick took flight over the fence right towards her. Poor Mary, half out of her mind by now, was at the far end of the Giddings's yard. She would have been unable to lift the stick, let alone throw it. Four pails of water traveled back and forth across the fence, but only one pail spilled. How anybody could be keeping track at that point, is a good question. Neighborhood women flocked to the Giddings's house to see what in the world was going on over there. The befuddled Mrs. Giddings sent Mary to the tannery to bring George W. Allen and his brother Rufus Allen, owners or the Wisconsin Leather Company, to the house. The two gentlemen arrived promptly bringing with them, Dr. Meacham and Dr. Nathaniel A. Gray, a Milwaukee obstetrician.

A lot of good that did. George Allen tried to bring calmness to the situation, but the stove-lid lifter, which is an iron handle, flew off the wood stove, bolted ten feet through the air, and struck Allen's leg. A pie with a yen for traveling flew past him and smashed against the stove. Allen hastily departed.

Mary sweeps the floor

Hired to help in the boarding house, Mary was asked by Mrs. Giddings to sweep up the floor, which by this time had formed a collage of broken dishes, glass shards, splintered wood, and tasty food. Dr. Meacham kept an eye on the frightened girl. He had a bird's eye view of Mary and the pantry. As Dr. Meacham was observing, and trying to stay out of target range, a small china dish sailed horizontally out of the pantry. He successfully managed to avoid being hit, and the dish landed on the floor, spilling the cards it contained, but remaining in one piece.

Becoming overwhelmed with the idea that sweeping just was not going to do much in the way of cleaning up all the mess, Mary began to wash the floor. But even pails of water misbehave under these circumstances. The soapy water seeped to the edges of the room and into the now large crowd of onlookers who could not believe what they were experiencing. Mary ended up chasing the pail only to be struck on the head by a flying bowl with a departure flight from the pantry. The men in the crowd searched the pantry, the kitchen, and the dinning room for *anything* that could be propelling the objects. Nothing.

Reporters get wind of the commotion

By now, it was late afternoon and reporters had arrived, prepared to interview anybody and everybody. Of course, some folks had decided this was literally too "off the wall" to hang around. Each witness was interviewed independently to determine whether there had been collusion on the reports or not. Since the phenomenon occurred only in Mary's presence, it was thought that perhaps she had thrown the objects. The witnesses' scrupulous observation and the extraordinary journeys of the objects pointed to Mary's innocence. The conclusion, as determined by highly trusted eyewitnesses, was that the events had occurred "without human agency."

A reporter who talked with the child observed her to be "a pitiable creature fearful of staying in the house or doing anything." Mary had no explanations for the events of the day. The thorough reporter also learned that Mary sometimes arose in the night to fight off "imaginary enemies." Mrs. Spiegel, Mary's mother, who could not speak English, was in the room at the time of the news interview, and concluded that the newsman must be a policeman or a detective, and that he was gathering evidence to charge Mary with witchcraft. A little panic ensued, and Mrs. Spiegel vehemently scolded Mary. The child trembled and cried as she curled up and sank into the chair.

That evening, Mr. and Mrs. Giddings reluctantly decided that they could not keep Mary in their employment, and instructed her to return home. Mary begged to stay, but ended up hiding in the woodshed. Her father found her and beat her once again, severely.

Mary attempted suicide by trying to drown in the river, but an unnamed gentleman rescued her. He took the shivering girl to the Giddings's house. Young Mary said she tried to take her own life because she could no longer tolerate the brutality of the beatings and the torment of the life she was leading.

Still a touchy situation

Mr. and Mrs. Giddings once again sent her back to her parent's house, but this time sent a dish of food along. Mary returned the empty dish the following day, but things started to happen again. She placed the empty dish on the table, and the teapot crashed from the stove to the floor. The teapot was now damaged beyond repair. The Giddings, who logically wanted to avoid further tornados, forced Mary out of the house.

By now, Mary had unwittingly caught the attention of Dr. Chauncey C. Robinson, a prominent Milwaukee physician.

He took Mary back to the Giddings house to question Mrs. Giddings about the situation. The doctor and Mary arrived as the borders and the Giddings were eating dinner. Knives and forks launched from the table.

According to news reports of the day, Mary was ultimately taken into the home of a physician in the Seventh Ward in Milwaukee. "Experts" at the time concluded Mary was "neurotic," but they could not pin down a reason for the paranormal activity that clung to Mary.

Today's Explanation

Parapsychologists would say Mary's was a case of poltergeist activity. This kind of activity is by definition "paranormal," in the sense that it is out of the ordinary, but normal in the sense that anomalies of energy like this happen, and can be attributed to the workings of the mind and electromagnetic energy. The explanation today is that a child, usually an adolescent female with emotional disruption in her life, can cause such phenomena. Often times, the child is unaware that she (or he) is the cause of it. When the child is removed from the situation, or sometimes when the child seeks mental health counseling, or just grows out of it, the paranormal activity ceases. This kind of activity can happen with adults and young children, but it is most common in adolescents. It might not have anything to do with spirit entities or ghosts, but people tend to lump it into that realm.

The British Jesuit scholar, author, and investigator of psychic phenomena, Herbert Thurston (1856-1939) included this case in his book *Ghosts and Poltergeists* (Chicago, 1954). He labeled it a "remarkable American case." Truly, it is.

Information on this case comes from the book Haunted Wisconsin *by Beth Scott and Michael Norman,* Ghosts of the Prairie *by Troy Taylor,* Milwaukee Journal Sentinel *and* Marianland Roman Catholic Resource.

The Steamer Chicora:
Beauty of the Great Lakes

Ships on the Great Lakes always come equipped with tales, especially if they go under with the best of them. The prized *Chicora* was dressed in mahogany and cherry woods, and had a grand speed of seventeen miles per hour. She was launched in Detroit in 1852. The 217-foot passenger and package freight steamer routinely made trips between Milwaukee, Wisconsin and St. Joseph, Michigan on lower Lake Michigan. The vessel was a sturdy and efficient ship that attracted a lot of business.

The *Chicora* normally hibernated during the winter at St. Joseph. Winter storms on Lake Michigan are fierce. In January of 1895, the *Chicora* awoke to be put into service. An unusually late grain harvest happened in the fall of 1894, and surplus flour stored in Milwaukee needed to reach the market. The flour had to be transported from Milwaukee to St. Joseph where it could be loaded into 40 boxcars. The trip to get across Lake Michigan this time of the year was a gamble.

John H. Graham of Graham and Morton Transportation Company took the gamble that it could do two or three runs provided the weather held stable. Captain Edward Stines, age 42, an experienced seaman who had worked for the company for 25 years took the assignment. Captain's son, 23-year-old Benjamin, was hired as a temporary second mate. William J. Russell, the regular second mate was ill, and could not make the journey. Usual crewmembers had taken other jobs during the winter months. James R. Clark was the replacement clerk, and a friend of his, Joseph Pearl the druggist from St. Joseph, made the trip too.

On the trip from St. Joseph to Milwaukee, Pearl managed to enrage Captain Stines when he shot a duck that had landed on the *Chicora.* It was a strange phenomenon to see a duck so far from land in mid winter. The Captain was horrified, and he believed the act of shooting the duck signified an evil omen. The story about the duck was published in a *Milwaukee Journal* story on January 24, 1895. Oddly enough, the Captain had thought of canceling the whole trip that fateful January 21 day because he was ill and had consulted a physician who advised that he not make the trip. He agreed with the doctor, but changed his mind at the last minute.

Warning: Duck with Barometer

Fear about the wasteful shooting of the duck spread amongst the crewmembers. When the vessel was loaded in Milwaukee, the captain was so obsessed with his belief of the evil omen duck that he talked about it to other people on the dock. It was 4:00 A.M. when John Graham, the ship's owner, looked at his barometer at his home in St. Joseph, Michigan. The barometer reading was 28, extremely low. The ship, now in Milwaukee, was to set sail for Michigan that very morning. John Graham wasted no time in racing down to the docks and ordering his other ship, the *Petoskey*, to stay in St. Joseph. Graham sent an urgent message by telegraph to be delivered immediately to the *Chicora*. But it was too late. The ship was pulling away from the dock, and nobody heard the shouts of the bike courier, "Telegram for Captain Stines!" It was 5:00AM.

Stines probably saw the barometer that morning also, but it would have been hard to predict when the storm would hit. However, the ship actually was especially built for running on ice. Insurance was not available for the ship because operating it in the winter was too risky. Stines likely thought he could make the seven and one-half hour trip before running into the inclement weather. An hour later, *Chicora* was in trouble, and by 9:00AM, the storm had reached 60-70 mph winds with blinding snow, and ice accumulating on the decks.

Waves peaked at more than 20 feet high. The temperature dropped 40 degrees, and for two solid days, the fierce storm clutched the ship in its grasp.

Gone Missing

The ship did not arrive at St. Joseph. Initially, this was of little concern. The local men thought she had returned to Milwaukee or took shelter in another port. The ship was reported seen in different locations, sheltering behind an island, disabled and adrift north of nowhere. John Graham sent frantic telegrams to ports along the route, in hopes that the ship took refuge at one of them. On January 24, 1895, a telegram from South Haven, Michigan, about 35 miles north of St. Joseph, read: "port side and forward upper bulwarks five feet wide and twelve feet long, inside shutters to passenger gangway all belonging to the *Chicora*, were found this morning about a mile out on the ice."

The most notable sighting, however, was off Chicago on Sunday, February 3. The Graham and Morton Company received a telegram stating the hull of the *Chicora* was floating seven miles out and that there were nine survivors. Tugs rushed to rescue, but when they arrived, the wreck was gone. Yet others claimed they could still see the wreck and that people aboard were waving hats. The observers said there were 15-19 survivors.

The tug *Protection* sighted a dark form of Hyde Park, and the captain thought it could be the hull with men moving on it. It turned out to be an iceberg with seagulls and ducks. The mystery of what the Chicagoans were seeing has never been solved. Some insist it was the missing steamer. Others say the captain was right—just birds and ice.

The tugboat *Crosby* and the steamers, *City of Ludington*, the *Petoskey* and the *Nyack*, went looking for the "gone missing." They too hoped to find survivors on chunks of floating ice. The team found curtains, decoration, cargo, planking

The ghost ship *Chicora,* which sank in Lake Michigan in January 1895. A message in a bottle told of the ship's fate. (Illustration by Hannah Heidi Levy)

and two spars, barreled flour, but no survivors and no bodies. Reports said that the ship's dog was found alive on the beach at St. Joseph a few days after the shipwreck. A story recounts years later, a cloth cap with a G&M on it was found on the beach, with a skeleton hand still grasping it.

Witnessing the demise of the *Chicora*

Sad accounts came from observers on the shore. Some say they saw the *Chicora* go under in the torrent. Henry Gross, age seventeen, reported hearing a ship's whistle blowing repeatedly at a point seven miles below South Haven. Residents of South Haven reported seeing lights of a vessel, and then the lights disappeared. Witness William Hare reported seeing the freighter near South Haven. "Her stern was down, and she appeared to be sinking. There were no spars, and I saw no signs of life, nor did I hear any disaster signals."

The final hours of the *Chicora* are summed up in two cryptic notes found floating in bottles. The first note read:

All is lost. Could see land if not snowed and blowed. Engines give out, drifting to shore in ice. Captain and clerk swept off. We have a hard time of it. 10:15 o'clock.

The second note was found sealed in a glass preserving jar:

Chicora *engines broke. Drifted into trough of sea. We have lost all hope. She has gone to pieces. Good bye, McClure, Engineer.*

Ghostly sightings of the *Chicora*

Crewmembers on the car ferries of Lake Michigan have reported sighting a ghost image of the *Chicora*. The steamer has been seen a few miles off the bow of the ferries, but it disappears quickly. After seeing the *Chicora,* the crews say that they get ready for a "hell of a blow." One famous *Chicora* sighting occurred in 1926. A ship, traveling across Lake Michigan in a gale and snowstorm spotted a floundering steamer from the pilothouse. The wooden steamer was blowing distress blasts, dead ahead.

The captain swung clear of the steamer, and then turned back to render aid. The snow was blinding and dense. The lost ship was nowhere in sight. He frantically tried to relocate it, but failed. The captain hastily reported it to the Coast Guard at the Straits of Mackinac. The description of the wooden steamer did not match any vessel that sailed the straits. The Coast Guard had no knowledge of such a ship in existence.

One veteran chief led the captain down the hallway into another room, and pointed to a faded picture on the wall. "Is this the ship you saw?" he hesitantly asked the Captain.

The captain studied the old picture. "There's no doubt, that's the one," he said.

The Coast Guard chief told the captain that the ship in the picture was the *Chicora* that sank in 1895 in the same area the captain had seen the apparition of the old freighter. "You're the first person, I've ever met who has seen the *Chicora*," said the chief. "I've heard of others. Are you sure you want to make this report official?"

"Chief, I know what I saw," said the captain. Bravely enough, the captain stood by his claims, but reportedly came close to losing his sailing ticket, as it was thought that he was crazy or drunk.

Information for this piece came from Haunted Lakes *(1997) by Frederick Stonehouse, and* Ghosts of the Great Lakes *(2003) by Megan Long.*

Mary Buth Farm
Germantown

The Germantown farmhouse was 140 years old at the time—old enough to contain its share of history. Tom Walton and his family were working on New Year's Day preparations on December 31 when little things out of the ordinary began to happen. The house suddenly felt cooler for no reason. A small candle burned faster than an identical candle next to it. The television lost power a couple of times. All of this would be easy enough to brush off as minor glitches for the day, but outside the living room window stood a not-so-minor glitch. An older woman in a rough-looking black dress stared at the festivity going on inside. Then she simply disappeared.

John and Mary Buth built the farm and homestead in 1838. The cabin was used as a trading post for early settlers and traders. Native Americans camped by a stream near the property. A section of the original log cabin is part of the two-story frame house that sits on the property today, and log-ceiling beams support an area of the second floor of the house. The original Buth family consisted of three children. Mary Buth, was the only daughter, and was named after her mother, Mary. The daughter died at age 76 in 1926 and was unmarried. The ghosts of the mother and daughter are said to haunt the Buth farm, roaming the farm property by day, and inhabiting the house at night.

Tom Walton and his family moved into the farmhouse in 1961 and paid little attention to the tales. But on that December 31, in 1965, Tom began to scratch his head and think that perhaps he would give more credit to the lore now that he had spotted the apparition at the window. On January 1, Tom found that the pepper plant near the window where he had seen the woman had wilted leaves on the window side and healthy leaves on the other half of the plant.

Other strange occurrences added to the suspicion that the

farm was haunted. A guest talked about seeing a young girl in the yard, but she vanished into the morning mist. Another time, Tom heard a violin playing in the house. The stereo was turned off, and no radio was playing. Was it the son, Herman Buth, again playing his music? A plumber working alone in the house on the kitchen heard footsteps coming from the upstairs.

A psychic, Mrs. Leader, was called in to try to help determine what entities were sharing the farm with the Walton family. Mrs. Leader determined that at least two ghosts were present, the mother and the daughter. The younger Mary Buth lurked outside looking for a lost lover, and she was considered an "evil" entity. A local tale says that Mary was left standing at the alter on her wedding day. The older Mary inhabits the house and supposedly protects it from the daughter. Some neighbors in the area don't buy the psychic's revelations and say that the younger Mary ended up an old maid, and perhaps a little eccentric, but had a good heart, cared for mentally handicapped, and would hardly be wanting to haunt the old farm. The mother Mary died at age 93 in 1899.

The long-time residents of the area reported that Mary and her brothers worked hard on their farm, maintaining it and offering their farm as a resting place to peddlers traveling from Milwaukee and other parts of the state. Some speculate that an itinerant peddler proposed to the young Mary and then took off to greener pastures before tying the knot. The Waltons moved from the farm in 1976, at which time the John Ewens family moved on to the property. The Ewens are aware of the ghost stories, and the neighborhood children are reluctant to visit the place because of the alleged haunting. Tom Walton still wonders about the strange cluster of occurrences that happened on December 31, 1965, but he decided a long time ago, that the ghosts were part of life at the farm. To this day, the farm is still known as the Mary Buth Farm.

Bedroom Curtain Ghost
Milwaukee

It happened on Hill Street. Dan Connell sat in the front room on this day in Septmeber 1878. He was mourning the death of Mary Tubey, his young stepsister. It was early afternoon. The door to his bedroom was open, and he had a clear view of the window in the room. Was it just a shadow, or was that actually Mary's face on the curtain? The longer he gazed at the face on the curtain, the clearer it became. Dan called to his wife to have a look at the curtain. She saw the same thing. Trying to play it off as imagination or patterns in the fabric, Dan and his wife tried to stay busy that afternoon. Curiosity nagged at them, however, and they continued to check on the curtain. Were the two imagining things? The peaceful face was always present every time they looked.

Neighbors caught wind of the face in the curtain, and they flocked to the house in droves. They all looked at the curtain; some saw nothing and laughed; others saw the face. A police officer visited the house at 3:00PM and stated that he had definitely seen the face. It was in plain sight. Dan and his wife were tired of having their house invaded so they refused to accommodate any more people. The following day, the crowds were back and numbered in the hundreds to file past the curtain. The face disappeared around dusk that evening. A reporter called on Mrs. Connell a week later. He also interviewed many of the neighbors. All were adamant about the existence of a face on the curtain. The reporter decided to leave well enough alone, and did not try to rebuke the story.

Restless Spirit Footsteps
Milwaukee

The hallway and both stairways were carpeted in this older Milwaukee house on the west side on Upper Wells Street between 25th and 26th Street. Dr. Gerhard Bading and his wife were renting the house in 1908. The couple decided to take a trip that year, and asked a friend, Dr. E.J.W. Notz to occupy the house in their absence. Dr. Notz moved in and had no problem falling asleep that night. It was shortly after midnight that he heard a thundering crash and footsteps running down the rear stairway. Dr. Notz quickly turned on the light and searched the attic, the first and second floors and the basement. He was convinced that somebody was in the house. He found nobody and no clues as to any kind of entry to the property. Dr. Notz returned to bed and fell asleep.

Crash, and then hurried footsteps across the hall, and down the stairway, woke the doctor once again. Dr. Notz repeated the search and found nothing. Then it happened for a third time, and was definitely getting on the doctor's nerves by this time. The second night in the house ended up to be a repeat performance of the first night. Dr. Notz asked one of his relatives about the situation, but still he gained no explanation.

The story goes that the house was haunted by the ghost of a servant girl who committed suicide on the property. The servant had been sent to the house early on a fall day to prepare it for the arrival of its owner, a resort hotel proprietor from the Waukesha Lake Country area. The servant girl had been suffering from depression. After she arrived at the house, she killed herself. She has since roamed the hallways and stairways, and has managed to frighten every family or individual who has lived at the house.

Ramada Plaza Hotel
accommodates extra guests
Fond du Lac

The Ramada (Retlaw) Plaza located at 1 North Main Street in Fond du Lac has a hauntingly fine reputation. The building built in the Prohibition era of the 1920's remains in tact with its neoclassical revival architecture. Original crystal chandeliers grace the hotel. The place has been described as a "heavy duty poltergeist playground." Reportedly, a woman employee was preparing for an event in the ballroom when she saw a green glowing light form in the room. She screamed for help, and her co-worker came to assist. He tried to brush at the light with a broom that he grabbed, but nothing happened until he threw the broom at the light, after which, it vanished. You'd think that would have been enough fright for the evening. Well, hardly.

That evening the woman employee screamed again, but this time it was from the women's locker room. Again, co-worker Dan rushed to her aid, and found that all the locker doors were rattling simultaneously. Apparently, both employees decided this was a tad too paranormal, and they fled the building. The following day, the woman resigned from the job. Resigning from the haunted hotel is not an extraordinary event.

As in many hotels, the management folks like to know what you thought about your stay there as a guest. Many curious excerpts are in the hotel's collection.

November 18, 2003, from "A Trip Advisor User in Wheaton, Illinois" states:

A very nice hotel with lots of charm, but this place gave me the creeps. An older couple on the way up to the seventh floor (the floor we're both staying on) told me this hotel had a haunted past, and I didn't believe it...at first. But in the middle of the night, I heard noises coming from the bathroom, so I went to investigate and found nothing. While in the bathroom I heard footsteps coming from the room near the bed, but when I looked I also found nothing. Then later that night I awoke again, feeling like I was being held. Weird! Supposedly this place has a history and I'm curious if something bad has happened in the old place over the years....

November 22, 2002 from "A Trip Advisor User" states:
A good hotel, but something sat down on my bed in a dark room — and I was alone! I was later told other guests had had unusual experiences.

August 4, 2003 from "A Trip Advisor User, Waukegan, Illinois" states:
Ramada was a very nice Hotel. Service was good and the building is very clean. I had a very warm feeling there, like staying at a well-kept comfortable home. One drawback was an odd occurrence that woke me one night. I felt a hand resting on my chest while I was sleeping. It felt like my mother used to do when she would try to calm me down at night. It brought back a pleasant memory, but it left me a bit on edge after that. My room was secure and I have no doubt it stayed that way all night. No explanations.

A few years ago, a hotel guest and several housekeepers heard a man screaming on the seventh floor. Bill, a maintenance employee rushed to Room 717 where he had heard "Help me!" coming from the room. Bill saw the door moving outward as if being kicked from the inside. He quickly called the front desk to see who was registered in the room, and was told that nobody was registered for the room, and the female guest that had been there checked out hours before this. The noise stopped and Bill entered the room. It was empty. Bill expected to see marks on the door from the heavy banging, but there were none. The seventh floor seems to be a favorite ghost place as indicated by several occurrences such as this.

Why all the fuss? Supposedly, the owner of the hotel, Walter Schroeder was murdered on his property, and he now haunts the hotel. Employees who have seen his photo declare that the apparitions are of Walter. Phenomena include turning on faucets and lights, banging on walls, and screaming. The hotel keeps a log of occurrences and to date they have three, one hundred page books that have documented the incidents dating back to 1923. The hotel has underground tunnels on Main Street that lead from the Dillinger-era speakeasy across the street to the hotel where Milwaukee and Chicago gangsters frequently stayed. It's been said that when the speakeasy was raided, patrons would escape through the tunnels under Main Street that connected the illegal establishments to the hotel.

An unnamed ballerina is said to haunt the ballroom. Elevators that were supposedly "locked down" when the building was empty have moved to other floors with assistance from nobody. Kitchen staff have witnessed syrup bottles fly off the shelf, as well as glasses and dishes that rattle. The ghost is a fan of C-Span, and the housekeeping staff is called out on occasion because of complaints of a very loud TV or buzzing alarm clock in rooms that have not been occupied for days.

Short Stories in a Long List

Touring with the Cliff Notes

1. Almond (Portage County): Spiritland Cemetery got its name because the ghost of Dewit McLaughlin's wife would appear to him on a regular basis when he visited the cemetery. McLaughlin was an early settler. Contrary to rumor, Ed Gein, psychopathic grave robber, is not buried here. This cemetery may have been the site of at least one of his grave robberies.

2. Amery (Polk County): Amery Lutheran Church or East Immanuel Lutheran Church is a Norwegian church built around 1870, and is said to have a phantom congregation that holds services late at night. Whispering voices are heard coming from the inside walls of the building as well as from the wooden pews. Sounds of a group of people laughing and talking in the sanctuary or having a potluck dinner in the downstairs have been heard by many parishioners. The bell of the church began ringing on its own in 1981, and was first observed by the pastor Reverend Elizabeth Robinson. The bell continues to ring on its own frequently.

3. Annaton (Grant County): The town of Annaton **itself is the ghost.** It has been referred to as "Wisconsin's Brigadoon." The tale is that the town exists in another plane and reappears on occasion with its buildings and inhabitants.

4. Appleton (Outagamie County): Hearthstone Mansion is officially the Hearthstone Historic House Museum and is said to be haunted by A.W. Priest, a philanthropist of his era. Priest died in the home in 1930. Today, the office manager of the museum greets Priest the ghost by saying, "Good morning, Mr. Priest" every day. People in the museum have heard sounds of sneezing and have felt Priest's presence. The house itself is interesting in that it maintains its original Edison light fixtures, and it was the first residence in the world to obtain its power for lighting through a centrally located hydroelectric plant.

Appleton (Outagamie County): Zuelke Building on College Avenue has a cleaning crew whose ghost report includes an incident where one of the crew was cleaning one night in 1996 when he felt a tap on the shoulder. He turned around immediately and witnessed a half body and a hand fade into the wall. Another incident tells of a reception held in the building in 1990, during which a pianist was hired to play on a second floor balcony. The pianist took a break and all the elevators simultaneously stopped working. When the piano music resumed, the elevators were working again. Irving Zuelke, whose ghost is thought to haunt the building, was a pianist compassionate about music. Some believe his spirit was at the reception in 1996.

5. Augusta (Eau Claire County) Bridge Creek Township: Green Eyes Bridge has an interesting tale. The story goes that a man in Augusta murdered his family and then hanged himself on the bridge over the Eau Claire River. The ghost has been haunting the bridge for over 100 years. At night, glowing green eyes can be seen near the bridge. However, according to an entomologist, this could be the glow of firefly larvae. The legend persists saying that the eyes are seen in winter when there are no larvae. One person reported that in 1994 or 1995 she stayed in a cabin near the bridge with a group of friends. They drove into Augusta one day, to find that when they returned to the cabin, they found ropes tied into nooses and a strange shadow draped over the piano. The group left immediately, without taking their belongings, and never returned to the place.

6. Avoca (Iowa County): Winny Beaujeau is the **French-**

man's Ghost who was a French Canadian trapper working in the area. The tale comes from around the Avoca area. He is often associated with the Morey Creek Medicine Woman. The ghost is also known as "Frenchman", "Frenchie", or "the Frog." He can change form, and can be in human or animal form. The Frenchman ghost is rumored to be a "thief ghost" who hauls his treasures to an underwater cave. He's also a trickster ghost.

7. Baraboo (Sauk County): Highway 12 Hitchhiker legend is about a guy dressed in a green jacket, and he has black hair and a beard. If you're driving, and pass the hitchhiker, don't be surprised when you see him a mile further down the road. If you stop to pick him up, he disappears.

Baraboo: The Old Baraboo Inn: Flying dishes, a floating broom, pictures flying off the wall, a woman's voice, a piano playing and a saloon girl dancing. These and many more strange occurrences at the Old Baraboo Inn have led both the owner and patrons to believe it is haunted. The Inn, which is now a restaurant and bar, was once a brothel, established in 1864. Several sudden deaths have occurred on the property, including three prostitutes and two former owners. Untimely deaths are believed to be the forerunner of unsettled spirits who may not know they are dead, thus causing paranormal activity to occur.

One such death was that of a prostitute named Mary, who bled to death in the early 1900s. A customer claimed to have seen Mary dancing on the bar's dance floor, and a waitress has seen her behind the bar. The current owner, B.C. Farr, has heard a woman repeatedly calling his name. Farr claims that if the spirits don't like you, they will shut the door and turn off the light when you are in the basement cooler. Temperamental ghosts are exactly what every place should have.

8. Bethlehem Road (Iowa County): Tommy Lee Ghost is described as a hunter, fisher, and a trapper who tends the woods in the area.

9. Blanchardville (Lafayette County): School House

Ghost south of Blanchardville on highway 78, occupies an old red brick schoolhouse with a bell tower. Sometimes the ghost appears daily for a week, and then will disappear for months. It is thought that the ghost may be active at other old schools too, just as if he were an itinerant schoolteacher. The ghost has a teacher-ish routine in that he starts at about 4AM lighting the kerosene lamps. It is said that a glow appears in the windows of the schoolhouse. Next, the smoke rises out of the chimney, and the noisy pump handle creaks when the ghost fills a water bucket.

10. Blue Mounds (Dane County): Blue Mounds Watcher is a well-known ghost in Dane County who is a sentinel standing guard. Supposedly, he has a calming effect on people. Rumor has it that the ghost was a man who was shot in the head at Wisconsin Heights. Others say it is somebody brought back from Bad Axe for burial. Yet other stories report the watcher as a ghost of murder victims on Military Ridge Road.

11. Browntown (Green County): Browntown Thresher Ghost is a farmer ghost. One report says the ghost can be seen along Zander Creek east of Browntown. The ghost is cutting marsh hay in the meadows. Many people who worked on the train crews spotted the ghost, since it was easier to see from the railroad tracks than from the road. The ghost is a tall, thin figure in patched clothing with a broad-brimmed hat blocking the face. He wears a yellow bandanna tied around his neck.

12. Castle Rock (Grant County): Bohemian Ghosts are in northeast Grant County. They are also referred to as old country ghosts. Big Nose, Winter Man, Dirty Pants are some of the names of such ghosts. There is a ghost for every holiday and event such as weddings, funerals, and so on. The ghosts are considered similar to guardian angels.

13. Chippewa Falls (Chippewa County): Sheeley House was originally a boarding house, and now is a restaurant and saloon. The ghostly activity includes the sound of footsteps walking up and down the stairs at night after closing. Other phenomenon includes a mural of roses on the wall that keeps appearing even though it is painted over, although this is probably not a supernatural phenomenon. Another situation involved an employee locked in the freezer without explanation. He was able to pick the lock and free himself. The staff reported spoons falling from the air and landing on the floor in the dinning room. The saloon has a wall with a stenciled border of "S's". When the workers were finished renovating, they assured the owner, Jim Bloms, that all the "S's" were still intact when they finished, however there is now an S missing from the stenciled border.

14. Clark County Charlotte Mills Bridge: Charlotte Mills committed suicide on October 4, 1907 near a bridge that crosses the Black River. The bridge is on County Road H, but has been replaced twice since this incident. Area residents believe her ghost walks the bridge around the month of October. She is thought to be mourning the deaths of her two sons who died in the month of October. Several old reports from area farmers of the time claimed that they saw mists and strange lights hovering over the bridge. In one instance, a farmer's horse also saw some image and refused to cross the bridge.

15. Darlington (Lafayette County): Courthouse Ghost in Darlington supposedly began inhabiting the place while it was still under construction. One resident said the Lafayette County was a conglomeration of secret societies, and he talked about a group called the Knights of the Golden Circle, who were pro-Confederates. Supposedly, the courthouse ghost is derived from a person who had fallen victim to a lynching by the Golden Circle. The ghost can be seen in the upper windows at night, or walking around on the ground floor of the courthouse.

16. Dodgeville (Iowa County): Graveyard Ghosts were reported at the corner of Union Street and Clarence. In early lore, the graveyards reportedly showed screaming face apparitions and swinging corpses in the trees. The trees were cut down, and today, different crops of ghosts are pranksters, often showing up at community events. In the 1830's, 1840's, and 1850's a number of young people died in epidemics, so it is said they are making up for lost time.

Dodgeville (Iowa County): Subway Restaurant Ghost seems to be active. The rumor is that things fly off the shelves or fall to the floor, a foul odor saturates the building at times, the beepers that are on the door sound off, and employees report hearing their names called. There have been reports of a woman around 50 years old who stands by the cash register glaring at employees and then disappearing. Some believe the ghost of Mrs. Forbes, a former owner who was killed in a car accident, haunts the place. Since the year 2000, strange things have taken place. Employees reported that stacks of cups would fall over, and employees would turn their back to get something, and the sandwiches that had not been cut, were suddenly cut.

17. Eau Claire (Eau Claire County): Banbury Place was home to the Uniroyal manufacturing plant. According to reports, there was a tenant in one of the buildings growing marijuana. He died of an accidental electrocution as he tried to hook up an air conditioner. The tenant's body was found two weeks later. The haunting reports include sounds of moaning, screaming, and the hum of an air conditioner. When Chad Lewis and Terry Fisk were hosting their radio show *The Unexplained* from WOLF 108 FM studio in Banbury Place, a disk jockey reported seeing a ghost. They write in their book, *Wisconsin Road Guide to Haunted Locations*, "She was working alone in the studio with the outside door locked. Through the studio window, she glimpsed a man wearing a red shirt and walking down the hallway. Later she looked up and saw him standing on the other side of the window starring at her. Suddenly, he walked through the window and wall, came towards her, and passed through her body. She reported feeling a sensation of hot and cold, but was unharmed."

Eau Claire (Eau Claire County): Alex of Fire Station 10 is supposedly a former firefighter who died in 1981 at the age of 77. The haunting began shortly after Alex Blum's death. Apparitions of Alex have reportedly been seen by about 80 percent of the firefighters at that station. Pots and pans fly from the wall and heavy metal doors open and close by themselves. One incident involved an electrician who was working at the station when he felt a hand tap him on the shoulder. He turned his head and saw a hand that vanished. The electrician quickly left the station, leaving his tools behind.

18. Egg Harbor (Door County): Shipwrecked Brew Pub is home to the ghost of a stern woman named Verna Moore, who walks through the dining room. She has been spotted by employees and customers, and has been seen both upstairs and downstairs. Verna is said to keep an eye on the place, and her presence is an indication that something bad is about to happen, but she is considered a gentle spirit. The Shipwrecked is a restaurant and hotel. Customers who rented rooms reported hearing faint crying of a child, and seeing a young mother anxiously searching for the child. The mother is said to be one of Al Capone's women who had an illegitimate child. The fate of the mother and child are unknown, but they seem to have disappeared under questionable circumstances.

The attic and the roof of the establishment seem to have their own curious ghost. Employees had seen the ghost of a young man standing in the attic, but with the remodeling of the attic, the ghost has moved to the roof. Calls have come in from residents to the restaurant to report a person on the roof, but when the owners check the roof, nobody is there. The young man is said to be another child of Capone's who wanted to turn Capone into the authorities. Rumor has it that this son was murdered. Another ghost who hangs out at the place is an irritable old man, perhaps a lumberjack who was murdered at the Shipwrecked in the late 1800's.

19. Elk Creek (Dunn County): Mary of Elk Lake Dam

is the story of a young woman hitchhiking across Wisconsin. Mark K. Schlais was found on February 15, 1974 after being stabbed to death and pushed out of an orange or gold compact car. This is a cold case file and is still considered open. The legend is that the ghost of the young woman has been seen along the river under the dam, and sometimes she is spotted along the road near the bridge. The young woman appears to be glowing white. Virginia Hendricks (now deceased) lived near the dam, and stated that Mary would visit her often. The ghost always appeared in a pink angora sweater and white capri pants. She appeared to be a 20 year old and identified herself as "Mary." The apparition appeared at the same time every morning and afternoon through Virginia's garden, and would tap on the window. No one but Virginia has seen the ghost in this form.

20. Evansville (Rock County): Weary Bridge is where a death supposedly occurred while a young man was "car surfing." Another version says a carload of teens was killed after speeding around a corner and driving off the bridge into the water. Last, but maybe not least, another tale says the body of a boy was found hanged on the bridge. So what happens at this place? Reports include mechanical problems with cars, shadowy figures moving across the road or following people, unexplained scratches on people's bodies, the presence of orbs, a green glow at the end of the road, and phantom trains, cars, and motorcycles. Don't forget to count the imps, or little demons, that hide in the trees.

21. Fifield (Price County): Holy Cross is a road off of Highway 13 between Fifield and Phillips. The legend tells of a woman killed by a train at the railroad crossing who now haunts the area. Her apparition is seen over the water of a small pond near the tracks, or on the tracks themselves. She is said to be protecting others from her fate. Curiously, gnomes are said to play around the tracks, and when people throw rocks at them, the gnomes throw them back. Ghost children play in the field, and cold spots are experienced even on very hot days.

22. Fond du Lac (Fond du Lac County): Historic 1856 Octagon House in Fond du Lac is said to have a young boy roaming the house in apparition form. The present owner says he hasn't seen this, but remarked that strange things have happened in the house. For example, he stepped out of the room for a very brief time, and returned to find the spinning wheel disassembled. Objects are often moved and misplaced. The house was used as part of the Underground Railroad, contains nine passageways, a secret room, and an underground tunnel.

23. Genoa (Vernon County): Whiskers Olde Tyme Inn reports having a ghost of former owner, Kenneth Beck, haunting the place. Kenny watched CNN and kept the TV tuned only to that channel. Sometimes when current owner, Patty Ziegler, closes the place at night, she returns in the morning to find the television, stereo, lights, grill and coffee maker all turned on. About half of the dinner plates and several glasses have disappeared. The TV, when on a different channel, will frequently switch over to CNN.

24. Glenbeulah (Sheboygan County): Glenbeulah Graveyard is one of the most mentioned cemeteries in Wisconsin. Its official name is Walnut Grove Cemetery, and rumor has it that it was featured on *Unsolved Mysteries* and ranked as the third most-haunted place in the world. However, according to Chad Lewis and Terry Fisk, those two claims are false. The legend tells of a man who hanged himself in the graveyard and whose decapitated head rolled into town. The ghost can be seen wandering the cemetery after midnight. What people have reported are apparitions, including that of red-ish white people. Other claims say that one of the graves glows in the dark, lights appear, noises are heard, and a pair of shoes materializes on a grave.

25. Grafton (Ozaukee County): Ferrante's Grafton Hotel is now an Italian-American restaurant where people hear footsteps following them in the basement where apparitions have also appeared, music plays upstairs when nobody is there, and cabinets open and close by themselves. The manager of the Historical Grafton Hotel stated that there are strange occurrences; however, the staff believes that the spirits are friendly and nobody minds having them around.

26. Green Bay (Brown County): Downtown YMCA has it resident ghost in the form of a man in his 20's who was reported murdered, and now has been seen on the second floor of the building. It's said that the young man does not notice other people in the building and goes about his business. The YMCA used two floors for housing prior to 1980, and apparently three deaths occurred in the building around then. One person died of smoke inhalation when he returned to the burning building to retrieve his wallet, another person was stabbed to death in the hallway, and the third person was shot to death while watching TV.

27. Hartford (Washington County): Granddad's Bakery has been reported to have a ghost that bakes. Apparently, there is rumor of a secret underground passage from the bakery to the City Hall, which probably has significance to the history of the building.

28. Hartland (Waukesha County): Millevolte Recording Studio is said to have "Harvey" the ghost who is named after the huge disappearing white rabbit in the film of the same name. The owner of the studio, Vinny Millevolte, stated that he was able to record what he believes is something paranormal during a session. The heart beat sounds showed up on one of the tracks; however, nobody was playing that particular sound. Vinny also said that he could sometimes hear strange noises like doors creaking, footsteps on the stairs, or something going on in the kitchen.

Hartland (Waukesha County): Hartland Inn was a hotel and restaurant in the early 1900's. Today, only the restaurant is in operation. One night after closing time in 2002 or 2003, the busing staff was folding napkins around table 9 when they heard a horrible scream coming from the basement. One of the staff went down to the dark basement and found nothing. None of the staff had been in the basement when this occurred. Sightings of a little girl in a Victorian style sailor outfit have occurred in the basement from time to time.

29. Hayward (Sawyer County): Hayward's Ghost Island is uninhabited or is it? It is said that a photo of a ghost was taken near this island by a fishing guide and his client. The two men noticed a mist that appeared to have human form. The fishing guide snapped a picture on his Polaroid camera, and estimated the size of the misty figure to be 12-15 feet high. Fires and mysterious lights have also been seen on the island. People who pass the island get an eerie feeling.

The name "Ghost Island" was coined by Barb McMahon about 30 years ago. She and husband Bill own Golden Fawn Lodge in Hayward. A number of guests reported paranormal activity such as voices and strange sounds coming from the uninhabited island. The guests of the lodge inquired about who lived on the island, and had questions about mysterious lights and campfires. They noted a feeling of being watched from the island. There is no camping allowed on the island. An orange light hovers in the woods and moves sporadically through the woods according to Bill, Jr. He also reported having trouble with his boat batteries when near the island.

30. Hollandale (Iowa County): Ghost Wagons and teams of horses run along Highway 191 at night. Sometimes the wagons are driverless and horseless. If the drivers are onboard, they are sometimes seen as skeletons, and at other times are dressed in their Sunday clothes. There are several stories about the Hollandale Ghost Wagons and their drivers.

31. Hubertus (Washington County): Fox and Hounds Restaurant has a previous owner, Ray Wolf, who is said to haunt the restaurant after closing. Ray's paintings are on display, and a painting near the fireplace shows hunting dogs with ghosts hidden in the pictures. His best-known paintings are of circus life and its personalities. The building is partly original log hunting cabin. It's said that the lower level bar, the Rathskeller, is always cold and eerie. Ray acquired the cabin and its surrounding acres in 1929 for the price of one Tennessee walker horse and a "valuable old book."

32. Kenosha (Kenosha County): The Rhode Opera House on 56th Street: Who says that ghosts don't enjoy the theater? The Rhode Opera House in Kenosha is the home to many a ghostly tale. They range from patrons claiming to see an unidentified man, a ghost, sitting near the back of the theater, to audible occurrences; such as cast members who hear sounds of laughter, talking, and piano music. Some phenomena have even been caught on video tape. Strange occurrences led to the belief that the theater is haunted. One such occurrence is that of a stage crewmember claiming to have seen and felt a presence during a performance. He described this presence as a "cold, black cloud that passed through him." Another tale that has arisen is of a young girl seeing pretty ladies backstage. No one else could see the ladies. Was this a young child's imagination or a ghostly presence in the Opera House that only the sensitivity of a child could pick up on?

33. Kewaunee (Kewaunee County): The historic Karsten Inn: On the shores of Lake Michigan stands the three story red brick Karsten Inn on Ellis Street that is a resting and vacation spot for many, and the permanent home of Agatha, William, and Billy. Agatha, a maid at the Karsten Inn from 1921 to 1937, seems to hold such strong ties to her former calling that she still oversees the daily activities. Both guests and staff at the Karsten Inn have experienced cold spots in the former maid's quarters. The sound of Agatha sweeping still fills the hallways. William Karsten, the former owner, makes his presence know through his odor which is that of an old man in his former living quarters. He has even been known to move furniture when something upsets him. It has been said that women have felt a man starring at them while in the Inn. Could this be William?

34. Linden (Iowa County): Linden Mine Ghost early

in the 20ᵗʰ century could be heard pounding against stones in the southwest side of the village. Legend has it that one miner buried another miner alive after a fight over a baseball game where there was much betting and high stakes. The miner was unconscious but was taken for dead and then buried. His pounding was supposed to be a signal that he was still alive. The ghost is a dirt-covered figure, who drifts down the road, but he has not been seen since 1918, and the hammering continues.

35. Manitowish Waters (Vilas County): Little Bohemia is a resort located in Manitowish Waters off Highway 51. Allegedly, the resort is haunted by a victim of John Dillinger. Many staff and guests have reported unknown voices calling out, and items gone missing. Some have seen apparitions. Dillinger and his gang were known for their bank robberies in the Midwest, amongst other crimes. They rented rooms at Little Bohemia. Because of the firearms carried by the gangsters, and their wearing of notable attire, the gangsters were recognized by the owner, who in turn alerted the authorities by sending messages on matchbook covers to relatives.

The Chicago bureau of the federal Justice Department made a surprise visit to Little Bohemia where their sting operation went awry. Three Civilian Conservation Corps workers were mistaken for Dillinger and the gang. The workers were fired upon, causing injury to two and death to one.

The Dillinger gang got into a shootout, but escaped through the woods. Bullet holes are still visible in the lodge. Ghostly happenings include hearing strange voices and noises in a particular cabin that has now been made into a game room. Guests in the cabin claim to see apparitions. A cook at the resort stated that several items would be misplaced by unseen forces while he worked

36. Menomonie (Dunn County): Mabel Tainter Theater is thought to be haunted by the Mabel Tainter's ghost. The theater was built by the parents of Mabel after the death of the nineteen year old. The theater staff agrees that strange phenomena happen there, but they don't think it is the ghost of Mabel. Reports of lights in the room used as a library and storage room, reports of seeing people move about in the building when nobody is occupying it, security alarms tripped, and apparitions of a lady in white are all attributed to the haunted theater. An employee quit after seeing an apparition pass by him on the second floor of the theater. The theater is used today for the performing arts.

37. Mill Creek: Mill Creek Hermit stories focus on the north end of Evans Quarry Road. The stories vary widely and there are many versions. The hermit has been reported as hunched over and howling. It was said the hermit was a sorcerer. One person said the ghost lived in a cave off Ridgeview Road.

38. Mineral Point (Iowa County): Salesman Ghost of Mineral Point is associated with many hotels and places to stay. He sold patent medicines. **Stableboy Ghost of Mineral Point** is associated with High Street and with the Prairie Springs Hotel south of the county line on Highway 23. He resembles a boy of about twelve years old and he carries a horse collar and driving harness over his shoulder. **Triple-Decker Outhouse Ghost** haunting consists of boards rattling and moaning. Triple-decker outhouses were attached to the exterior of hillside boarding houses. **Pastor's Ghost** is associated with a traveling pastor thought to be a Methodist who stopped at many inns. He wanders and sniffs the smells of restaurants, and casts disapproving glances into tavern windows. **Bounty Hunter Ghost** is a stalking ghost on Ridge Street, and was an Englishman sent to retrieve a fugitive, but the Englishman died at the inn before he caught the runaway. **Traveler Ghosts** never made it out of Mineral Point, and one still roams the area, robbing wash lines of ladies' lingerie.

Mineral Point: Walker House Ghost (or Hanging Ghost or Caffee's Ghost) is seen on Water Street and associated with the Walker House. William Caffee was hanged in 1842 for the death of Samuel Southwick, which happened in an argument.

A crowd of 5000 people gathered to witness the hanging. It's been said that William Caffee came to the hanging along with his coffin while beating a funeral march out with empty beer bottles, but that cannot be verified.

The Walker House has been party to doors slamming, doors swinging, doorknobs rattling, and banging pots in the kitchen. The ghost is most active when he has a crowd around, and is described as defiant and angry. Owners and workers experienced hearing heavy breathing and footsteps. One worker, Calvert Walker, a chef at the restaurant heard strange noises and had little pranks pulled on him allegedly by the ghost. Calvert stated that he saw the ghost from 1978 through 1982, and that the ghost was wearing an old gray suit circa the mining period. It is interesting to note that in 1984, an exorcism was performed to rid the restaurant of seven spirits. People say the ghost of William Caffee remains today.

39. Mount Ida (Grant County): Hitchhiker is a modern ghost whose habits are up to date in that he is thought to be post World War II. He is seen as a neatly dressed young man who is hitchhiking, and has been seen more frequently in recent years. Most sightings are on Highway 18 between the north and south branches of Highway K. Legend has it that he is trying to free himself from this area, and will when he finds the people who killed him.

40. Nashotah (Waukesha County): Corner House Tavern is said to be a site of paranormal activity. Employees have witnessed cold spots and other things.

41. Nekoosa (Juneau County): Greenwood Cemetery has its very own Shadow Resident. The story goes that in October 1961 at dusk a group of teenagers parked their car near Greenwood Cemetery. A howling came from the cemetery as the iron gate swung open on its own. The three teenagers claimed to see a shadowy figure appear and disappear amongst the headstones. The figure was said to stomp on a new grave as the howls turned into screams. Not wanting to stick around any longer than necessary, the teens dashed back to the car and drove to a local bar where they found some other friends. Soon there were two cars of friends heading back to the cemetery to check out the claims. They saw nothing extraordinary at first with the exception of the gates still being open. However, in one corner of the cemetery was the groundskeeper storage shed with the shadowy figure inside. The howling began, the teens ran to their cars in record speed, and just got the heck out of there. Fact or entertaining legend concocted by imaginative teenagers?

42. Oconomowoc (Waukesha County): La Belle Cemetery (Lac La Belle Cemetery) has a large statue of a young woman standing in front of a huge cross. Supposedly, the hands of the statue drip blood and people have witnessed an apparition of a girl walking from the statue and drowning herself in Lake (Lac) La Belle. Other claims say that the statue has been associated with mysterious deaths, blindness, and other disasters. Another story says that the statue has come to life, walked down the stone steps, and into Fowler Lake. The statue itself is exquisite and was sculpted from Barre (pronounced "bury") granite by an unknown Italian sculptor from Barre, Vermont for the Nathusius family in the 1940's. Coins and other objects are sometimes placed in the hands of the statue by people who visit the gravesite of the Nathusius family.

43. Oshkosh (Winnebago County): New Moon Café is a coffee shop that can add several ghosts to its list of patrons. Originally, the building was a hotel called the Beckwith, after Sanford Beckwith, and it was destroyed in 1875 during the Great Oshkosh Fire. The hotel was rebuilt in 1876. A woman named Mrs. Paige died in this building in a fire in 1880. She was the wife of a wealthy lumberman. A few of the staff of the New Moon Café have encountered the ghost of Mrs. Paige downstairs. The ghost of a young man dressed in a bellhop uniform has been reported by many people also. Another ghost is that of a well-dressed elderly sophisticated woman. She appears in the main lobby.

Oshkosh (Winnebago County): Starseed is a new age shop located in the historic Beckwith block of downtown Oshkosh. Customers have sighted a vanishing phantom cat in the upstairs level of the building and near the second floor steps. Many children have also reported playing with a mysterious young child, and the staff has seen apparitions. The young child apparently died accidentally from a fall when he or she ran after a ball that was tumbling down the stairs.

44. Pecatonica River (Iowa County): Pecatonica Fisherman is seen in early morning mists in spring and summer. He is older, wears wire-rim glasses and has a white beard. The ghost is seen fishing or with a string of fish. He has even been seen fishing in a dried up creek by one observer. The ghost has been seen in many other counties besides Iowa County.

45. Phillips (Price County): Concrete Park on State Highway 13 is a popular place to visit, where some say the statutes move at night. Fred Smith's Outdoor Concrete Park has visitors who think they see actual people dressed up as statues moving about. Strange noises, shadowy figures, and apparitions have been reported. The 200 sculptures created by self-taught sculptor Fred Smith, include cowboys, miners, soldiers, Indians, and wild animals. Abe Lincoln, Ben Hur, Paul Bunyan, Sacagawea, and the Budweiser Clydesdale horses also reside in the park.

46. Plainfield (Waushara County): Clark's True Value Hardware is allegedly haunted by a former owner of the store, Bernice Worden, who became a victim of serial killer Ed Gein. Apparitions of the ghost are reported by employees and customers. The ghost carries order forms and speaks about anti-freeze. On the day of her death, Ed Gein apparently said he needed anti-freeze. When investigating a trail of blood in the store that lead out a back door, the sheriff found a receipt for anti-freeze. A horrific scene was discovered shortly afterwards at Gein's house. Bernice had been gutted and decapitated.

The property of Ed Gein is supposedly haunted also. No

house stands there today. People in the area claim to hear strange noises near the woods, and see mysterious lights. Gein told children in the area that his house was haunted. **Plainfield Cemetery** where Ed Gein is buried, and where he used to rob graves, is thought haunted and populated by restless spirits. The grave marker is in a Wautoma museum to prevent problems with theft. *Note: Please be considerate of the local townspeople if you visit the store or the area. They are sensitive about the topic, and are reluctant to speak of the atrocities.*

47. Pleasant Ridge (Grant County): Pleasant Ridge Peddler Ghost is thought to be the ghost of a peddler who was murdered for his goods. The ghost is seen loading a mule and is mostly seen on Highways Z and ZZ. The peddler and the mule have glowing red eyes. They bleed from wounds and have knives sticking out of them. The peddler clutches his neck to stop the flow of blood, and he can be seen on the road at night.

48. Portage (Columbia County): Wisconsin Street has a lady dressed in early 1900's clothing who appears to walk down the street with a stroller around 9:00PM. The apparition disappears when people approach. The Ghost Experts, Chad Lewis and Terry Fisk tell us that stating a specific time for the appearance of the woman is a sign that the story is local folklore rather than haunting. Downtown employees have not seen the apparition.

49. Potosi (Grant County): Potosi Brewery Ghost is said to be a German brewmaster who left the brewery when the business went under, and haunted the people who ran the brewery out of business. The brewery is also allegedly haunted by the former owner, an Englishman who often had disagreements with the German. Workers blamed the English ghost for equipment failures, ruined batches of beer, and whole railroad cars with barrels of beer disappearing.

50. Prairie du Chien (Crawford County): Treaty Ground Ghosts are seen in groups of three or four, but larger groups are common. Legend is they started to appear after the imprisonment of Black Hawk. One source believes they are from the Villa Louis site. The ghosts are sentinels against greed and corruption.

51. Reedsburg (Sauk County): Rag Lady is seen on Old Ironton Road and Schutte Road. The ghost drives a wagon down the road around late May or early June a couple times a year. It's interesting to see carpets, egg crates, and bundles of rags piled up in the wagon. The lady wears a broad-brimmed hat and coveralls. She supposedly leaves small gifts on the back porch.

52. Rocky Arbor (**Sauk County**): Rocky Arbor Battle Ghosts are thought to roam the area because of a battle fought between the natives and the Vikings. The battle lasted several days and ended with the downfall of the Vikings It was a bloody battle and many people were fatally wounded. Ghostly activity includes sounds of clashing clubs and axes, and loud whoops.

53. Sinsinawa Mound: Manido is the spirit of the mound. Odd happenings are reported. Many people do a pilgrimage to the mound. Manido is a Native American term.

54. Soldiers Grove (Crawford County): Civil War Phantoms are large groups of soldier ghosts found in Soldier's Grove. They are characterized by fading in and out of their "camp." They have been spotted playing cards, singing, and drinking. Some have reported that amputee phantom soldiers dance at the camps.

55. Stevens Point (Portage County): Black Bridge is the location of an alleged ghost searching for her lover who died at the mill near the Black Bridge. The bridge is a train trestle that crosses the Wisconsin River below the Point Dam in Stevens Point.

Stevens Point (Portage County): Blood Cemetery also known as Woodville Cemetery or Linwood Town Cemetery, is the location for the origin of the tales of Calvin Blood who hanged himself in a tree in the cemetery. Another tale says he was an infantry deserter during the Civil War, and after caught, was hanged in the tree that overlooks his grave. Yet another tale says Calvin Blood was a young boy who died from a blood disease. The fact is that Calvin Blood died at the age of 81 of tuberculosis. He was a Civil War infantryman, and was buried in the cemetery. Rumors tell of the tree that bleeds, and people having mechanical problems with their car including over-heating and interior lights flickering on and off. It has been said that strong winds blow inside the cemetery, but not outside. Strange blue lights chase people. *Note: Trespassing is prohibited.*

Stevens Point (Portage County): Bloody Bride Bridge on highway 66 brings the tale of a young bride who was killed on her wedding night in a car accident on the bridge. However, there exists no record of such an occurrence. The lore is rather typical scary ghost stuff. Supposedly, a police officer was driving over the bridge and saw an apparition of the young woman standing in the middle of the road. He thought he hit the woman when he was unable to stop in time. The officer immediately stopped his car and looked back to see what had happened. As he did so, he found the Bloody Bride sitting in the backseat of the squad car.

Stevens Point (Portage County): Boy Scout Lane is so-called because the land was owned by the Boy Scouts, and it was supposed to be the location of a campsite.

The rumor is that a troop of Boy Scouts on a camping trip was murdered here in the woods by the bus driver. Another version says they Scouts dropped a lantern and accidentally set the woods on fire, killing the other troop members. The ghosts of Boy Scouts haunt the road and swing a lantern on dark nights.

Stevens Point (Portage County): Old Swenson is the name of the ghost who supposedly haunts County Road 11 in Linwood Township. The ghost carries a bouquet of flowers, and looks for the grave of his wife. He is floating and missing his legs. People in the area report that a worker named Swenson or Swanson worked for the Soo Line in the early 1900's, and was killed in a railroad accident that severed both legs. He was not buried next to his wife, but continued to look for her. It's curious as to where the stories come from since there are no railroad tracks or cemeteries on County Road 11.

56. Washington Island (Door County): Nelsen's Hall, **home of the Bitters Club** is allegedly haunted by former owner Tom Nelsen. Tom was a pharmacist and built the hall in 1899 to serve as a community center. He introduced the custom of drinking 90 proof Angostura Bitters as a tonic to aid the stomach. He was able to "dispense" this stomach tonic throughout Prohibition, and thus keep his bar open. Nelsen's Hall is the oldest legally operating saloon in Wisconsin since it was granted permission to conduct business as usual during Prohibition.

Ghostly activity includes phantom footsteps leading upstairs to an apartment, and an apparition in the women's restroom. A bartender working one night heard somebody ask for a glass of water, but when she turned around, nobody was there. She has seen glimpses of an apparition passing through the room. Another bartender closing up and finishing work in the kitchen, heard the radio turn on by itself, and at the same time, the station switched from rock music to country western music. Co-owner Doug lost part of a finger when a window that he was cleaning, came crashing down on his hand. Was the ghost responsible for this window-finger mishap?

57. Wisconsin Dells (Columbia County): Showboat Saloon is the setting for "Molly" who supposedly lived upstairs. Her haunting activity seems to be harmless and begins after 3:00 AM. Upstairs doors open and close without assistance, and if someone is cooking upstairs, the ghost has fun with the appliances. People wearing late 1800's clothing have appeared in the mirrors of the saloon. Voices are heard near the stage, and cold spots are felt in the cellar. Kegs of beer are also rearranged. A feeling of nausea and anxiety overtakes some people when they go into the cellar. A previous owner of the saloon, Michael Showalter has noted that there seems to be paranormal activity in the place.

Wisconsin Dells (Columbia County): Dungeon of Horrors has its share of possible paranormal activity. Owner Bill Nehring says he has a difficult time retaining employees due to the situation. He claims the paranormal activity seems to occur mostly around August every year, especially during rainy and overcast days. Bill has owned the place for 24 years, and he estimates that the majority of his employees have experienced paranormal occurrences. It is a fact that in the late 1950's or early 60's the owner of the building, which was then a Ford garage, committed suicide in the place early one morning.

The employees have witnessed an apparition of an older man with glasses. The tales also tell of an apparition carrying an axe and following people, cold spots, orbs, and a partial hand materializing and then disappearing. Another rumor is that people have felt breathing on their shoulder when nobody was in the area, and that invisible hands grab people and hit them with invisible objects. Bill the owner had one experience where he felt something on his shoulder, and heard a static or crackling noise, while at the same time, an employee saw a glowing orange apparition. The static sound ceased as the orange glow disappeared.

58. Wisconsin Rapids (Wood County): Hotel Mead reportedly has the ghost of a woman bartender, who, rumor says, was stabbed to death in the Shanghai Room in the 1950's. Lights flicker and doors shut by themselves. The employees do not discuss things related to an alleged haunting. Chad Lewis and Terry Fisk continue to investigate the information about a female employee who was killed in the 1960's in an after-hours party.

59. Wisconsin River: Wisconsin River Cliff Ghost is the spirit of a woman who dwells around the Lone Rock Bridge on the south shore of the Wisconsin River. One legend has it that she was tricked by a river spirit to dive into the river where she drowned. She resembles the Lorelei of the Rhine River in Germany who lures boatmen into foolish acts. Rumor has it that she wanders a stretch of highway 133, crying as she goes.

60. Woodman (Grant County): Tim (Timmy, Timothy) the Ghost lurks around Rosendale Road and Shady Hollow Lane. He is a benign tramp ghost who helps lost children get home, and has been known to fetch help in an emergency, and perform other good deeds. Tim is thought to be a farm laborer who froze to death.

Here's Another Boat Load of Ghosts

Appleton --Dairy Queen
Appleton--Huntley Elementary
Appleton—Huntley School
Appleton--Old Catholic Cemetery
Appleton--Secura Insurance Company
Argonne --Old Argonne Grade School
Ashippin--Ashippin School (possible)
Ashland--Northland College Memorial Hall
Aztalan--State Park (Lake Mills)
Baraboo—Hwy 12
Bayfield--Michigan Island Lighthouse
Beaver Dam--Community Theater
Beloit--BeloitTurner School
Beloit--McNeel Middle School
Beloit--The Manor
Beloit--The Trestles on Riverside
Boltonville--Jay Road
Boltonville--Seven Bridge Road
Boscobel --Hotel Boscobel
Boulder Junction--Old Tavern
Boulder Junction--Stevenson Creek

Bowler--Bowler High School and Middle school
Broadhead--Flynn's Steakhouse
Broadhead--Hell's Playground
Brookfield--Dousman Dunkel Behling Inn
Burlington--Burlington Public Cemetery
Caledonia--Oak Creek Bridge on Boarder
Cameron--Betty's Café
Canton--Bantely Graveyard
Caryville—Old Caryville Church
Caryville—Old Cemetery
Caryville—Old School
Cederburg--Founder's Park
Chetek--Highway M
Chilton--Corner of Breed Street and State Street
Chilton--Wal Mart
Chippewa Falls--Sheeley House
Clear Lake--Moe Church
Coon Valley--Disciascio's Italian Restaurant
Cornell--Cornell City Library
Cottage Grove--Woods on Church Street off Rinden
Road
Crawford-Ferryville--Swing Inn
Crooked Lake--Pines Bar
Dane--Springfield Hill
Delafield—Nashotah House and Seminary
Delafield—St. John's Military Academy (house is Rosslyne
Manse)
Dodgeville—Subway shop
Eagle River—Dog Meadow Ghost Lights
Eagle River--Railroad Tracks
Eagle--Rainbow Springs Golf Course
East Troy--Cobblestone Bar
Eau Claire--Rope Swing downtown
Eau Claire--Stones Throw Bar
Eau Claire--The Opera House
Eau Claire--Univ. of Wisconsin—Kjer Theater

Eau Claire--Vine Street
Edgerton--Memorial Community Hospital
Eleva--Rachel's Field
Elkhart Lake--Lion's Park
Elkhorn--Peak Station Road
Elkmond--The Over Look Tower
Elm Grove--Sunset Theater
Evansville--East Side Steak House (Evansville House)
Fifield--Fifield Cemetery
Fifield--Fifield School
Fifield--Holy Cross area near lake
Fond du Lac--Galloway House
Fond du Lac--Octagon House
Fond du Lac--Ramada Plaza
Fond du Lac--St. Mary's Springs Seminary
Franklin--Whitnall Park
Genoa--Big River Restaurant
Germantown--Old Mary Buth House
Green Bay--Barid's Creek
Green Bay--Brewbaker's Pub
Green Bay—Downtown YMCA
Green Bay—Heritage Hill State Park
Green Bay—West Shirley Road
Green Lake—Dartford Cemetery
Greenfield—Whitnall Park
Hales Corners—Whitnall Park
Hallie—Eagles Club
Hartland—Recording Studio
Hartland—the Hartland Inn
Hayward—Lac Courte Oriellis Casino
Hilbert—Hilbert Road
Howard—Peterson House
Hubertus –Fox and Hounds Restaurant
Hudson—Paschal Aldrich Home
Janesville—Oak Hill Cemetery
Janesville—Olde Towne Mall

Janesville—Univ. of Wisconsin Rock County Theater
Jefferson—Paradise Road (Advice: stay out of the woods on left hand side)
Jefferson—St. Coletta's College, Serra Hall
Juneau—Eagle Road Cemetery
Kenosha—Durkee Mansion
Kenosha—Kemper Hall (Seminary)
Kenosha—Pleasant Prairie Paupers Cemetery
Kenosha—Rhode Opera House
Keshena—County Road VV
Keshena—Menominee Casino Bingo Hall
Kewaunee—Historic Karsten Inn
Kohler—Old Governor's Mansion
Kohler—The American Club
La Crosse—Bodega Brew Pub
La Crosse—Dells Bar
La Crosse—Old Holmbo Residence
Lac du Flambeau—Bingo Hall
Ladysmith—El Rancho
Lake Delton—Ringling Road
Lake Geneva—St. Killians
Land o lakes—Summerwind
Lowell—bridge
Madison—Bar Next Door
Madison—Bay View Townhouses (?)
Madison—La Follette High School
Madison—Maple Bluff Country Club
Madison—Memorial Union 2nd floor
Madison—Old Madison Jail
Madison—Orpheum Theater
Madison—Sanitarium Hill
Madison—Science Hall
Madison—State Capitol 4th floor
Manitowoc—Evergreen Inn Hotel 8th floor and Lounge
Manitowoc—Lincoln High School
Manitowoc—St. Mary's Nursing Home

Manitowoc—St. Nazianz JKF Prep
Maribel—Maribel Caves
Marinette County—Mclintock Park
Marshfield—Old County Hospital
McFarland—Dyreson Road
Menasha—Menash High School
Menasha—Valley Road
Menomonee Falls—Grace Lutheran School
Menomonee Falls—Main Street
Menomonie—UW Stout-Tainter Hall
Mequon—Concordia University WI
Meridian—Pavilion
Merrill—Hospital next to Scott Mansion
Merrill—Scott Mansion
Milton—High School
Milwaukee—Bell Middle School
Milwaukee—Cardinal Stritch University (dorms)
Milwaukee—Giddings Boarding House (1874) now a
private residence
Milwaukee—Grand Avenue Mall
Milwaukee—Old Northwest General Hospital
Milwaukee—Pfister Hotel
Milwaukee—River Hills- Milwaukee Country Club
Milwaukee—South Milwaukee Grant Park
Milwaukee—St. Adalbert Catholic School and Church
Milwaukee—St. Raphael School, South Campus
Milwaukee—Tamorack
Milwaukee—the Modjeska Theater
Milwaukee—The Pfister Hotel
Milwaukee—The Rave – Eagles Club
Milwaukee—Univ. of Wisconsin-Milwaukee, Sandburg
Halls
Milwaukee—Wisconsin Lutheran College
Minocqua—Tula's Café
Monona—Muskie Lounge& Crab House (4 Lakes Yacht
Club) (Jingles on the River)

Monroe—Idle Hour Mansion
Mukwonago—Heaven City Restaurant
Mukwonago—Inn the Olden Days
Nashotah—Hasslinger's Resort (area privately owned now)
Neekosa—Old Alexander Middle School
New Richmond—Kozy Korner Restaurant
Oak Creek—Bender Park
Oak Creek—Carolville-Peter Cooper Glue Factory (NO trespassing)
Oak Creek—Fitzsimmon's Road
Oconomowoc—Fowler Lake
Oconomowoc—Oconomowoc Highschool
Ojibwa—Rainbow Asylum Bar
Oneida—Norbert Hill Center
Oostbrg—Veterans Park
Oshkosh—The Grand Opera House
Oshkosh—The Paine Art Center
Oshkosh—Winnebago State Hospital, Sherman Hall
Oulu—Abandoned Saw Mill
Pipe—Club Harbor
Plainfield—True Value Hardware
Plover—Hyw 54-old abandoned house
Plover—Old Sherman Restaurant
Plymouth—Yankee Hill Inn Bed and Breakfast
Portage—Church Road (cemetery)
Portage—Wisconsin Street (lady)
Potosi—Brunner Food Center (downtown)
Prairie Du Chien—Wyalusing Academy
Racine—Dekoven Center
Racine—Elmwood Plaza (video store)
Racine—Microtel Inn and Suites
Racine—Northside Pick n' Save
Racine—Pritchard Park
Racine—Racine Country Club
Racine—SC Johnson Company

Racine—Westlawn Cemetery
Racine—Winslow School
Readfield—Cemetery
Rhinelander—five Sister Lakes
Rhinelander—Molly's Rock on Pine Lake Road
Rhinelander—St. Joseph's Cemetery
Rib Lake—Rib Lake Campgrounds
Ripon—Ripon College (Brockway Hall)
Rock Island—Rock Island State Park
Rosendale—Witch Road
Rusk—Ladysmith—Ladysmith High school
Saint Nazianz—JFK Prep School
Saint Nazianz—Society of Divine Savior Seminary
Schawano—Chicken Alley
Sheboygan Falls-Eagle River—railway tracks
Sheboygan—First Star Bank (downtown)
Sheboygan—Kohler—The American Club
Sheboygan—Sheboygan Yacht Club
South Milwaukee—Man Child's House
Spooner—Corral Bar
Spooner—Hammill House
Spring Green—Taliesen (Frank Lloyd Wright)
St. Francis—Marian Center (theater) (old school)
Stevens Point—Hyw 66 (Bloody Bride)
Stevens Point—Red Bridge
Stockbridge—Joe Road
Stoughton—Weary Road
Stoughton—Weary Road Bridge
Strum—Strum Cemetery
Superior—Fairlawn Mansion
Superior—Fairlawn Mansion
Tomahawk—Calvary Cemetery (on Hyw S)
Union Grove—house located on State Street next to high school
Walworth—Walworth Grade School
Wascott—Hunting Lodge

Washington Island—Gretchen of Range Line Road
Washington Island—Nelsen's Hall and Bitters Pub
Waterford—Tichigan Lake Inn
Waukesha—South High School
Waukesha—Tabernacle Cemetery
Waukesha—Waukesha Area Chamber of Commerce (old house)
Waukesha—Whittier Elementary
Waupaca—Simpson's Restaurant
Wausau—Rib Mountain Storage Plant
Wausau—Univ. of Wisconsin (hallways)
Wauwatosa—Eschweiler Building
Wauwatosa—Potters Field
Wauwatosa—Wauwatosa West High School
West Allis—Majdecki Sentry
West Bend—old Holy Angels building (now apartments)
West Bend—Univ. of Wisconsin Washington County (library)
West De Pere—St. Lawrence Cemetery
Westby—Fairchild's House
Weyauwega—Marsh Road
Whitefish Bay—Dominican High School (3rd floor and theater)
Whitelaw—Maplecrest Sanitarium
Whitewater—Univ. of Wisconsin (Center of the Arts)
Whitewater—Univ. of Wisconsin (Clem Hall)
Whitewater—Univ. of Wisconsin (Delta Zeta House)
Whitewater—Univ. of Wisconsin (Fricker Hall)
Whitewater—Univ. of Wisconsin (Knilans Hall and Wells Hall)
Wild Rose—Tuttle Lake (campsite)
Wisconsin Dells—Showboat Saloon
Wisconsin Dells—The Dell House
Wisconsin Rapids—Forest Hill Cemetery
Wisconsin Rapids—Mead Hotel

End of the Story
or is it?

Tips on Ghost Hunting

Ghost hunting and paranormal investigation are not quite the same thing, however, there's a heck of a lot less syllables involved when you're talking about "ghost hunting" vs. "paranormal investigation."(three vs. nine syllables, to be exact). If you're a ghost hunter, you may be taking photos in a cemetery on a dark night, or you're visiting some reportedly haunted place to experience the presence of the supernatural, either by seeing an apparition, feeling a cold spot when it's 85 degrees out, or just getting that sort of eerie, deep anxiety feeling of dread. Maybe you're just curious about the history, the folklore, and the reports.

A paranormal investigator, on the other hand, sets up shop with various pieces of equipment, and parks for the long haul to record audio, video, meter read-outs, and other kinds of documentation. The investigator's goal is to add to the study of paranormal phenomena as accurately, objectively, and scientifically as possible.

We're going to incorporate common sense with technical information, rules, and suggestions to use in whatever situation you may find yourself in, or embarking upon.

Our research has turned up handy sources of information, which include the work of Troy Taylor of the American Ghost Society, standards and protocols from the International Ghost Hunters Society, and guidelines from various researchers, some of whom are interviewed in this book. So, if you're going on a Ghost Hunting outing...

Standards and Protocols of the International Ghost Society

1.   Ask the spirits of the dead for permission to take their photos.

2.   Respect posted property, ask permission and do not trespass.

3.   Always conduct your investigations in a professional manner.

4.   Show reverence and respect in cemeteries, battle-fields, historic sites, etc.

5.   No running or horseplay in cemeteries or historical sites.

6.   Positive mental attitude is very important for all investigations.

7.   Skeptical minds will generate a negative energy during an investigation. Do not bring along skeptics or those who are negative and want proof that ghosts exist.

8.   Follow the lunar cycles and solar storms for conducting investigations for best results. Paranormal events occur during peak geomagnetic field conditions.

9.   Do not take photographs during adverse weather conditions, such as rain, mist, fog, snow, windy or dusty conditions.

10.   Remove or wear the camera strap so it does not hang loose.

11.   Take photos of dust particles, pollen, and moisture droplets to see how your camera records these kinds of orbs.

12.   An orb is not special or unique. An orb is only a description of shape. Most common orbs are airborne dust particles.

13.   Multiple orbs in photos are usually dust particles, not spirits.

14.   Do not take photos from moving vehicles on dusty

roads or while walking on dusty roads.

15. Remove all dust, spots, and fingerprints from camera lens.

16. Avoid shooting into the sun. This may cause lens flare.

17. Avoid shooting with flash at reflective or shinny surfaces.

18. Keep fingers and long hair away from the lens of the camera.

19. Avoid shooting when foreign objects are floating near the camera.

20. Compare anomalous prints with negatives for confirmation.

21. Flash is only good in a 9-12 feet range from the camera, so focus on that.

22. Always use fresh audio tapes for tape recordings.

23. If digital, record in one or two minute tracks.

24. After twenty minutes, the spirit will get bored; no need to record longer in one area.

25. Do not rub the side of the recorder or walk while recording. Stand still.

26. We do not consider Ouija boards, dowsing rods, pendants or séances valid investigation tools.

27. No smoking, drugs, or drinking during an investigation.

28. If people are angry, they should not be involved with an investigation. They will draw angry spirits, and the other spirits will avoid them.

Educational, enlightening, entertaining, thrilling...

...is how Troy Taylor, President of the American Ghost Society, describes ghost research. Troy says he won't have all the answers to the mysteries until he himself is a ghost. He has been actively tracking down the supernatural for nearly twenty years and has visited several hundred *allegedly* haunted locations. Troy emphasizes the "alleged" part of things because, as he says, "Probably 90% of those locations have perfectly natural explanations for the phenomena that have been reported over the years, but it's that remaining small percentage that keeps all of us coming back for more."

According to Troy, it's hard to define "haunted house." Churches, theaters, office buildings, libraries, graveyards, any building and any place can become haunted. The activity of unexplained happenings comes in the form of apparitions, footsteps, noises, odors, and so on. For a spot to be considered genuinely haunted, the phenomena must be directly related to the place itself. For example, if a place is truly haunted, and a family that lives there decides to move out, the next family who lives there should experience the same things the previous family experienced. Most often, ghosts are not seen in a haunted house. In the majority of cases, ghostly noises—footsteps, voices, mumbling, whispers, knocking sounds—are heard instead. In some cases, solid objects such as knick-knacks, or even furniture, move about by themselves. No two cases are ever alike.

Fabrications about ghosts and haunting abound. Ghosts are not "everywhere." In most cases, you have to go looking for them, because they are not going to find you. Ghosts are usually not out to kill anyone or avenge their deaths. The instances of harmful ghosts are so rare that the few cases that have been documented have been hugely sensationalized. They don't appear with white sheets draped over their heads, but are usually in a white-mist form that may resemble a person. In some cases, the ghosts appear solid, or life-like.

Haunted houses also come with standard misconceptions. Many people believe that only old, rundown, ramshackle buildings can become haunted, but even relatively new homes have been known to attract ghosts. Some people believe that ghosts cannot be photographed. This is another great misconception. Authenticated photos of ghosts are on record. It is quite important to note that just because a house lacks apparitions; it does not mean the house is without its ghosts. Going a step further, just because you have never seen a ghost, does not mean ghosts don't exist.

Belief in ghosts seems to have little or nothing to do with whether you see one or not. One part of the human perception uses the five senses, and the other part has to do with processing done in the mind. Supposedly, the brain only allows us to see what it thinks we can handle, so we keep adding and subtracting. There are individuals who seem to be "on a different wavelength," and have the ability to see things other people do not. It's possible that these people are "receivers" of an energy that most of us cannot see or sense. What we're saying here is that perhaps ghost sightings involve a perfectly natural energy that we simply do not understand yet. So, the question becomes, are ghosts seen as they really are? Troy Taylor says:

The conscious spirits are not…that's why photographs that have been taken of paranormal energy show balls of light, globes and strange mists. These photos probably show spirits as they really are. But what about when people see spirits wearing clothes? Residual impressions are going to be wearing clothes because they are not conscious spirits, merely an *imprint* left behind. Conscious spirits will sometimes appear in clothing because the people who are sensitive enough to see them can see the spirit as it once was. The spirit is "making contact" with that person, and the witness is seeing the ghost how it still sees itself…human-like and wearing the clothing they wore in life.

So, how can we prove ghosts exist?

A ghost can be defined as a disembodied personality or "mind." Presently, we have no physical evidence that the mind actually exists inside the body. To say it exists outside the body in the ether is another huge leap. By our observations, we infer that the mind exists. The closest we can come to proving ghosts exist is by gathering witness testimony, taking photographs, and documenting details. Reports from independent witnesses with similar experiences are considered strong evidence if the testimony comes from different periods in time. To prove absolutely and scientifically that ghosts exist, is probably not going to happen, because we cannot duplicate the results under strict research conditions. Ghosts don't make appointments to show up in the laboratory. Researchers have disagreements as to what a ghost actually is. Not everyone believes that a ghost is the spirit of the dead who has come back to haunt.

Why do people like to ghost hunt? For one thing, there's no "open season" and you don't have a "limit," and it's as Troy said, "educational, enlightening, entertaining, and thrilling." But the deeper part of this is that ghost hunters believe there are worlds of things out there beyond our understanding, and it might turn out that those who have an open mind about the "impossible" may be the ones who help find some answers. This is an activity for the patiently curious.

The most important tool in ghost hunting is you, the hunter. Every case is a cause for using wise judgment and your own powers of observation. Be prepared to find people who like to "pull your leg," or people who are somewhat strange or scared who erroneously believe their house is haunted. Ghost research does not demand forbidden or arcane knowledge, spells, or incantations to collect credible evidence of ghosts.

Ghost hunters have goals. They seek evidence of the paranormal, but they also are on board to help the distressed people who, for their own peace of mind, are searching for an answer, whether it is normal or paranormal. People are frightened. Explaining that the activity is strange, not evil or demonic is an important job of a ghost hunter.

Beware the bogus ghost hunter

A good researcher must never claim that evidence is genuine unless it is strictly and absolutely genuine. Good evidence should be strong and open to criticism by those who wish to challenge it. And then we have a word from Troy Taylor again regarding "pseudo ghost hunters"....

The pseudo-ghost hunters are the ones giving paranormal research a bad name, not the debunkers whom the public realizes will provide an argument for any valid point that exists. What happens is that the public mistakenly comes to believe that these sloppy ghost hunters must be representative of the entire paranormal community. Obviously, they are not. This group mostly consists of hobbyists who are too lazy to do proper research, have never heard of confidentiality in private cases, are far too "out there" with metaphysical theories to recall what planet they are on, or are simply too misguided or ill-informed to understand that camera straps in photos are not ghosts. There are no experts when it comes to the paranormal.

Don't believe every "investigation" that you run into on the internet. Many ghost hunters chase about and search for the "what's" and the "how's" of haunting, but they forget to explore the "why." Why is the location haunted? Why did the history of the place create a haunting? Why are the phenomena taking place? If you're just running around taking pictures, then all you're doing is, well…taking pictures. That's ghost hunting; that's not ghost research. To do research there must be an element of organization behind it, and there must be criteria to follow.

A word on skepticism

The word "skeptic" has been molded over the years to take on a somewhat negative charge, and to mean "close-minded" to everything. But the actual meaning of skeptic says that a skeptic is a person who keeps an open mind about everything. A good skeptic would believe in the possibility of ghosts, however, the skeptic also knows that not every ghost story has something to do with ghosts. A good descriptive word to use for the close-minded is "debunker."

My house is haunted...what should I do?

Good question...that's the first thing you want to say (or at least think) if you're the one trying to help. Seriously speaking, when people get to the point of believing their place is haunted, they can find themselves in an awful lot of distress. They're afraid to be alone, afraid to go in certain areas of the house, paranoid if the faucet starts leaking, easily startled at meaningless noises, hyper-vigilant, lacking sleep due to anxiety or gossip over the matter, and so forth. But, on the other hand, sometimes they're accepting of things, and they are calling you in because they're curious, or they want some kind of confirmation or reassurance about the situation.

Should they move out? Should they stay? Should they talk to the specters or ignore them? Should they call a priest or other professional? Should they invite the idea of contacting a ghost hunter? Should they call an electrician or a plumber? To start with, the witness of ghostly events has to think about whether these occurrences are natural or supernatural. Relaxation time outs and good observation are needed even in the presence of fear. You have to give it all a dose of rational thought. Was the "cold chill" just a draft after all? Match the events to an explanation if you can.

It doesn't take much to let the imagination run wild. A couple of seemingly harmless comments from someone in the household will get you a haunted house on the block. Mice in the walls are masters at creating frenzied thinking amongst the human population. Once you use haunting as your explanation for the common mouse sounds, you've pretty much created a monster. Because even though your place isn't haunted, the important thing is that you believe it is haunted. At this point, unfortunately, *belief* becomes *truth*. Whew! What a dangerous combination that is! Now every bit of creaking, every noise that sounds remotely like a footstep, and every shadow that becomes more than a shadow starts to run your life. And then your family joins the panic club. Bottom line is, remember to step back and use a calm, rational mind.

If you do call in an investigator, it should be one who does not accept things at face value—you want the skeptic, as defined in the previous chapter. Remember, it's not that the skeptic doesn't believe you. It's because the skeptic is working on keeping an open mind. You need that objectivity of the skeptic. But to save a lot of hullabaloo, you might want to call the electrician or the plumber first.

Keep a journal or a log of any event that occurs in the house that may be linked to this haunting situation—date, exact time, place, weather conditions, people present at the time, reactions of pets, other things in the environment such as a train passing by on the tracks, and so on. Have any other witnesses record their thoughts in the journal. If you call in ghost investigators, there are a few considerations to pay attention to carefully.

1. First of all, many websites that advertise as investigators exist—not every group is reliable. Make sure the investigators offer a real live phone number. An initial contact by e-mail is O.K. but you need a phone number.

2. Contact information on the ghost hunters' web site should list first and last names. If only first names are listed, it might not be a very reliable source—wishful ghost hunters.

3. Try to determine from at least the website if these are people you'd want in your home. If the website is questionable, so are the ghost hunters.

4. Avoid ghost hunters who dabble in magic, the occult or offer magical cleansings of homes. If anything like this appears on the website, then move on. Solid researchers do not employ these means.

5. Legitimate ghost hunters do not charge for any service. If a ghost hunter has to travel, it is legitimate that the person be reimbursed, however

6. Legitimate ghost hunters come to your home *invited.*

If you are contacted and asked if an investigation can be conducted in your home, run. However, if the allegedly haunted place is in a public location, that organization or people associated with that place may be contacted by a research group. Judge the group on their merits.

7. Once you've found an investigator or group that you believe is trustworthy, check the qualifications for an investigation. How long have they been involved in paranormal research? Ask about past investigations, especially those involving private residences. If an individual investigator claims to be some sort of "doctor," ask where his credentials came from. A questionable "doctorate" acquired from a questionable source, does not guarantee any kind of expertise or abilities. Many ghost hunters have never conducted investigations in a home, no matter how experienced they seem. They may turn out to be great investigators, but you have to decide if you want to be their first private home investigation or not.

8. Ask if your prospective researcher is affiliated with a group or national organization. Affiliation with a group with a good reputation can help you make a decision about allowing research in your home. Get in touch with the group by calling their main number, and check this person out.

9. You may have to be patient when requesting help. Legitimate researchers do not charge for their investigations, so you'll to wait until the investigator has some free time. Some shady organizations claim to "ghost bust" and charge large sums of money. Genuine investigators are interested in collecting evidence, not money.

10. The ghost hunter will ask a large number of questions. Be prepared to answer them. A lot of answers are needed in order to determine if an onsite investigation is warranted. The organization or individual will want to know what you've tried to do to rule out natural explanations for the phenomena, and they may want to see evidence of that in your logbook.

11. Prepare to have your house invaded by no more than five or six group members. An investigation will be invasive—

count on it. Photographs will be taken along with hundreds of feet of video. They will ask you (perhaps several times) to describe the events, and your answers will be recorded. Many of their questions will perhaps seem unconnected, and some questions may be embarrassing. Their questions have a purpose. They are working to legitimize your story and to determine if the activity is truly a haunting.

12. Good investigators remain noncommittal. They will arrive with skepticism. They must do this to look at evidence objectively.

13. Good investigators know how to use all of their equipment. Ask them about the equipment if there are things you want to know about or don't understand. Ask them what the equipment is used for in the investigation. If they can't explain it, you might have a problem.

14. Unless the investigation was set up through you with a television station or other media, the investigators should not have a reporter or media person in tow. Investigators keep aspects of your case confidential unless they have your permission to disclose anything.

15. Natural explanations that are discovered should be properly explained to you. This is not an indictment against your honesty. When you asked for an investigation, you also asked for an honest opinion.

16. Everyone in the household who experienced the unusual phenomena or events should be present during the investigation. Friends and relatives who are curious and want to watch the proceedings should be kept out. Their presence can be very distracting to you and the investigators, and can interfere with an accurate investigation.

17. If you become uncomfortable with any part of the investigation, you have the right to halt the investigation. Investigators must respect your feelings and fears.

18. Team members divide their duties. Some will be asking questions, others will be filming, taking photos, and mapping the house. They will want you to recreate what you were do-

ing at the time of the events. If the phenomena have a pattern, such as a set time of day when it occurs, the investigators will set up a "ghost watch" or vigil to try to document the activity. This can be long and boring, and you just might want to go on about your business quietly.

19. In most cases, a follow up visit will be required by the team. This is let painful than the first visit, since the groundwork has already been established.

20. A legitimate researcher will always follow up on a case, but don't be afraid to get in touch with the researchers and ask them to come back if the ghostly activity persists. Most people are not afraid of the activity that goes on, but they are bothered by it to the point of seeking some help.

21. If the place actually has some paranormal activity going on, you may want to call the proceedings to a halt. This can happen when the witness is afraid of "angering" the ghost. Do you simply want to leave well enough alone? Some people want to "get rid" of the ghost. Investigators are not equipped to eliminate ghosts. You will have to contact an outside source, but the ghost hunter can be proactive in helping you with your wishes. If you have a family minister or priest or other religious practitioner, the ghost hunter may suggest that you get in touch with this person. The minister may come to your house and pray for the soul of the spirit. This is not an exorcism, but rather an attempt to get the spirit to leave in peace. It can be beneficial for the family. Understand that ghosts are not present to hurt anyone, and in most cases, a family can peacefully coincide with a spirit.

22. If your religious person is not available, the ghost hunter might suggest or find an expert in getting rid of ghosts. They may not be a professional medium or psychic but someone who is sensitive to spirits and who has a good reputation. Either the ghost hunter has worked with this person before, or the person has been referred through a reputable source. There is usually a lack of ceremony with this person, as the person is not a phony psychic or exorcist.

Be cautious, however.

23. If an authentic medium detects a spirit, sometimes they can convince the spirit to move on, and sometimes not. The medium usually has a positive effect on the house, no matter what happens. Troy Taylor says, "I often get calls from people who ask for this service, but in my years in the paranormal field, I have found very few people that I can recommend as trustworthy enough to give this assignment. They are out there though, and if you request it, the ghost hunter will help you get in touch with them if they know of the resource."

Final note on this...

Man fears what he does not understand. The ghost hunter's goal is to collect evidence of ghosts, and to alleviate fear by helping the clients deal with the activity they are experiencing.

Information was taken from an essay, "American Ghost Research—What to do When Your House is Haunted," by Troy Taylor, President of American Ghost Society.
www.prairieghosts.com

Message in a Bottle

Writing this book has been fun, "educational, enlightening, entertaining, and thrilling," to quote Troy Taylor. We look at this book as a message in a bottle in the sense that this book is just pretty much out there for anybody who wants to pick up an interesting read or add a book to a collection of regional ghost books. Just like an old bottle drifting in vast waters, you might find this book by accident, and it might be years from now. But the book has a message here and there, although not quite as desperate as the classic message in a bottle.

Not to get too far off track (but we are talking about ghosts, and that's off track enough), bottled messages are a curious thing. Placing a message in a bottle just before a ship sank was an attempt (and probably most reliable way) of communicating a last word to the outside world. Although some messages were hoaxes, others were not. At the turn of the 20th century, brass "message tubes" were on board freighters for the purpose of saving a final crewmember list or other last message in the event of loss. The tubes were kept in the pilothouse, and ready for quick access. The practice of writing a message continued as late as November 10, 1975 when the *Edmund Fitzgerald* went under. In fact, when a crewmember on the *Arthur M. Anderson* learned that his ship was turning around to go back out and look for the *Fitzgerald,* he recorded his last words on an audio cassette and sealed it tightly in a jar…just in case.

Just as in this book, messages found in bottles need to be viewed with the context in which they are written. A bottle and a pencil and paper in the midst of a screaming sea and raging storm were hard to come by. The messages were brief and succinct. Above all, a message in a bottle was a last desperate effort to communicate beyond the reaches of another world. In this message, there was a desire to note what crew was on board, and why the ship was sinking. This was the last message from the car ferry *Milwaukee,* lost on Lake Michigan in 1929 with 52 souls aboard:

S.S. *Milwaukee*
October 22, '29, 6:30P.M.
Ship is taking water fast. We have turned and headed for Milwaukee. Pumps are all working, but sea gate is bent and won't keep water out. Flickers are flooded. Seas are tremendous. Things look bad. Crew roll about the same as last payday.

A.R. Sardon, Purser

Thanks

The authors of this book thank you for your curiosity. If you find a bottle floating on Lake Michigan or any other body of water, pick it up. If you're incredibly lucky, you may have found a treasure and a voice from a past century. Although, not in ghost form, a message in a bottle is haunting in its own right. Books are that way also — they have their own evocative messages that sometimes haunt us in perpetuity.

Acknowledgments

Many thanks to all those who helped in the interviews for this book. We'd also like to thank staff at the Bar Next Door, Bootleggers Supper Club, Mickey's, Jingles, also Cory Guessler, Amy Meyer, Mary Juckem—ms. walker, Marv Balousek, Mary Lou Santovec, friends, well-meaning relatives, Chad Lewis and Terry Fisk, Linda Godfrey, Richard Hendricks, Todd Roll, Shawn Blaschka, Jen Lauer, David Schumacher, Heidi Linden, Amy Tomlin, Dante, Kathleen Schneider, Troy Taylor, J.L. Adler for critique on occasion, Connie and Todd Lynch, Jack Grimm, Arthur Wille, Joy Grimm, Mary Hasslinger, Denis Boyer, A.M. Scharko, Judy, Robert Steeno for patience, and a couple of fairly cooperative cats.

Bibliography and Resources

Books

Boyer, Dennis—*Driftless Spirits* (1996)

Boyer, Dennis—*Gone Missing* (2002)

Gard, Robert E., and Sorden, L.G.—*Wisconsin Lore* (1987)

Godfrey, Linda, and Hendricks, Richard—*Weird Wisconsin* (2005)

Hivert-Carthew—*Ghostly Lights* (1999)

Levy, Hannah Heidi—*Famous Wisconsin Mystics* (2003)

Lewis, Chad, and Fisk, Terry—*Wisconsin Road Guide to Haunted Locations* (2004)

Long, Megan—*Ghosts of the Great Lakes* (2003)

Merck's 1899 Manual of the Materia Medica

Norman, Michael, and Scott, Beth—*Haunted Wisconsin* (revised edition) (2001)

Rider, Geri—*Ghosts of Door County* (1992)

Scott, Beth, and Norman, Michael—*Haunted Wisconsin* (1980)

Steiger, Brad—*Real Ghosts, Restless Spirits, and Haunted Places* (2003)

Stonehouse, Frederick—*Haunted Lakes* (1997)

Taylor, Troy—*Ghost Hunter's Guidebook* (2001)

Articles

American Ghost Society—"Ghosts of the Prairie-Haunted Wisconsin"

American Ghost Society—"Introduction to Ghost Hunting"

American Ghost Society—"Summerwind"
American Ghost Society—"What to Do When Your House is Haunted"
Buffalo and Erie County Historical Society—"La Salle and the *Griffon*"
Burlington News (Bufo Radio)—"Vortexes, Paranormal, Ghosts"
Fox and Hounds Restaurant—history
Ghost Magazine —"Ramada Plaza Hotel"
International Ghost Hunters Society—"Standards and Protocols"
Lake and Countryside Magazine (Scott Hunter Smith)— "Home Again"
Milwaukee Journal Sentinel Online—"Nashotah Farms Shows its Spirits"
Newmonth Magazine (Scott Dayton)—"Kewaunee's Haunted Hotel — The Karsten"
Shadowlands —"Haunted Places Index —Wisconsin"
Washington Island.com—"Early Washington Island History"
West, Sharon K.—"Ghost Ships Blowin' in the Wind"
Wisconsin Historical Society Press—"The Haunted Mansion and Pines — Scott's Mansion-Merrill"

Website, Internet and Other Resources
American Ghost Society www.prairieghosts.com
American Society for Psychical Research www.aspr.com/index.htm
Badger Books www.badgerbooks.com
Dante (contact author)

Hannah Heidi Levy www.hannah-heidi.com
Heidi Linden www.angelfire.com/wi3/heidikbook
International Ghost Hunters Society www.ghostweb.com/sp.html

Linda Godfrey www.cnb-scene.com/books.html

S.P.I.N. Stateline Paranormal Investigations of WI www.spinwisconsin.com/

Schneider, Kathleen—Middleton, Wisconsin 608-836-1935 ksmystic@mailstation.com

Southern Wisconsin Paranormal Research Group www.paranormalresearchgroup.homestead.com

Unexplained Research www.unexplainedresearch.com (see links on their site)

Wausau Paranormal Research Society www.pat-wausau.org/

Index

A

Adams County 110
Allen, George W. 177
Allen, Rufus 177
Almond, Wis. 194
Amery, Wis. 194
Amery Lutheran Church 194
Angostura Bitters 214
Annaton, Wis. 194
Appleton, Wis. 194
Arthur M. Anderson (ship) 237
Augusta, Wis. 195
Avoca, Wis. 195

B

Bading, Dr. Gerhard 190
Baraboo, Wis. 196
Barsanti, Mr. 155
Bar Next Door 33, 78, 86
Beast of Bray Road 42
Beaujeau, Winny 195
Beck, Kenneth 202
Beck, Rev. James Lloyd 166
Beckwith, Sanford 209
Beever, Pete 85
Belts, Larry 16, 17
Ben Hur 210
Bitters Club 214
Blackhawk War 136
Black Hand 155
Blanchardville, Wis. 196
Blaschka, Shawn 19, 23
Bloms, Jim 198
Bloody Bride Bridge 213
Blue Mounds, Wis. 130, 197
Bober, Raymond 150, 152
Bootleggers Supper Club 99, 104
Borton, Brian 12, 78
Boyer, Dennis 10, 115
Boy Scout Lane 213
Bristol, Wis. 164
Browntown, Wis. 197

Brown County, Wia. 203
Brumder Mansion Bed and Breakfast 33
Budweiser Clydesdales 210
Buffalo and Erie County Historical Society 140
Bunyan, Paul 210
Burlington News 165
Buth, John and Mary 187

C

Caffee, William 207
Canada Global TV Network 44
Capone, Al 78, 81, 87, 99, 103
Carver, Jonathan 151, 152, 153
Caryville, Wis. 24, 25, 30
Caryville Cemetery 29
Castle Rock, Wis. 197
Chicago, Ill. 86, 99, 147, 155, 168, 183, 193, 206
Chicago's Union Station 155
Chicora (ship) 181
Chile, country of 141
China, country of 93
Chippewa County, Wis. 197
Chippewa Falls, Wis. 197
Chippewa River 27
Civilian Conservation Corps 206
Civil War 212, 213
Clark, June Rose 168
Clark's True Value Hardware 210
Clark County, Wis. 150, 198
Coast Guard, U.S. 186
Columbia County, Wis. 211, 214, 215
Connell, Dan 189
Corner House Tavern 208
Crawford County, Wis. 211, 212
Cullis, William 139

D

Dane County, Wis. 197
Dante 72
Darlington, Wis. 198
Deaver, Janet 165
Delafield, Wis. 146, 165, 166
Delevan, Wis. 43

Detroit Island 140
Dillinger, John 103, 193, 206
Dingeldine, Mrs. William 144
Dining with the Dead 33
Dodgeville, Wis. 130, 198
Door County, Wis. 116, 119, 200, 214
Driftless Spirits 115, 120
Dungeon of Horrors 215
Dunn County, Wis. 25, 200, 206
Dunn County Sheriff's Dept. 30

E

Eau Claire, Wis. 25, 78, 199
Eau Claire County, Wis. 195, 199
Edmund Fitzgerald (ship) 141, 237
Egg Harbor, Wis. 122, 200
Elk Creek, Wis. 200
Ellison Bay, Wis. 117
Ephraim, Wis. 119
Europe, continent of 144, 168
Evansville, Wis. 201
Everybody Loves Raymond (TV show) 106

F

Falstad, C.H. 27
Famous Wisconsin Mystics (book) 77
Farr, B.C. 196
Feeney, Dick 28
Fehlhaber, Henry 156
Fehlhaber, Mary 156
Fentz, Ernest 144
Ferrante's Grafton Hotel 202
Fifield, Wis. 201
Fisk, Terry 24, 31, 199, 202
Fond du Lac, Wis. 191, 202
Fond du Lac County, Wis. 202
Fox and Hounds Restaurant 204
France, country of 168
Fred Smith's Outdoor Concrete Park 210
Frontenac, Comte de 137

G

Gard, Robert E. 129

Gein, Ed 194, 210
Genoa, Wis. 202
Germantown, Wis. 187
Ghosts and Poltergeists (book) 180
Ghosts of Door County Wisconsin (book) 127
Ghosts of the Great Lakes (book) 140, 186
Ghosts of the Prairie Magazine 154, 180
Ghost Island 204
Gibson, George 156
Giddings, William 175
Giddings's Boarding House 175
Gill's Rock, Wis. 139
Glenbeulah, Wis. 202
Glenbeulah Graveyard 202
Godfrey, Linda 40, 49
Golden Fawn Lodge 204
Grafton, Wis. 202
Graham, John H. 181, 182
Graham and Morton Transportation Company 181
Granddad's Bakery 203
Grand Theater 15, 20
Granton, Wis. 150
Grant County, Wis. 194, 197, 208, 211, 216
Gray, Dr. Nathaniel A. 177
Greenwood Cemetery 208
Green Bay, Wis. 137, 203
Green County, Wis. 197
Green Eyes Bridge 195
Griffon (ship) 137, 141
Grimm, Clark "Corky" 171
Grimm, Jack 171, 175
Grimm, Joy Hasslinger 175
Guessler, Cory 78, 99

H

Hahn, Mrs. Jacob 146
Hanover, Germany 142
Hartford, Wis. 203
Hartland, Wis. 203
Hartland Inn 203
Hartung, Craig 164
Hasslinger, Herbert J. 168, 175
Hasslinger, Mary 175

Hasslinger Moose Lake Resort 167,
    168
Haunted Lakes (book) 186
Haunted Wisconsin (book) 148, 162,
    180
Hayward, Wis. 204
Hearthstone Historic House Museum
    194
Helfaer Theater 163
Hendricks, Richard 40
Hicks, Jeff 157
Hille, Hulda 144
Hille, John 142, 148
Hille, Magdelena 143
Hille, William 144
Hillsboro, Wis. 120
Hinshaw, Arnold and Ginger 149
Holdworth, John 139
Hollandale, Wis. 204
Hollywood, Calif. 22
Holmes, Sherlock 61
Holsen, Elizabeth Hasslinger 174
Holsen, Ted 175
Horse and Hound Café 73, 76
Hotel Mead 215
Hubertus, Wis. 204
Humphrey Hall (Apartments) 163

I

Illinois, state of 110
Inside Edition (TV show) 43
Iowa County, Wis. 129, 195, 196,
    198, 204, 205, 207, 210
Irving, Washington 130

J

Janesville, Wis. 36
Jeopardy (TV show) 68
Jesus Christ 48
Jingles Coliseum Bar 95
Juneau County, Wis. 208

K

Karsten Inn 205
Kelly (ship) 139
Kennedy, Anita 147

Kenney, Ransome 147
Kenosha, Wis. 205
Kenosha County, Wis. 205
Kewaunee, Wis. 205
Kewaunee County, Wis. 205
King, Stephen 142, 150
Kluka, Bill 102
Kluka, Janet "Bunny" 103
Krause, Elder 144
Kriesel, Rose 172
Krueger, Karen 95
Kuechle, Mr. 155
Kuhtz, H.S. 146

L

Lafayette County, Wis. 196, 198
Lake and Countryside (magazine)
    73
Lake Country Reporter (newspaper)
    167
Lake Huron 138
Lake Mendota 147
Lake Michigan 137, 138, 139
Lamont, Robert 149
La Belle Cemetery (Lac La Belle
    Cemetery) 209
La Salle, Rene-Robert Cavalier Sieur
    de 137
Leader, Mrs. 188
Levy, Hannah Heidi 12, 175
Lewis, Chad 24, 31, 199, 202
Lincoln, Abraham 210
Linden, Wis. 205
Linden, Heidi 50, 56
Linwood Township 213
Linwood Town Cemetery 212
Lisle, Ill. 110
Little Bohemia 206
Lloydson, Mr. 156
Long, Megan 140, 186
Ludington, Mich. 183
Lynch, Todd 174

M

Mabel Tainter Theater 206
Madison, Wis. 78, 97, 147
Madison, Ga. 73

Manitoulin Island 138
Manitowish Waters, Wis. 206
Maple Grove Township, Wis. 127
Marianland Roman Catholic Re-
    source 180
Marquette University 163
Mary Buth Farm 187
Masuda Hall 163
McCormick Mansion 147
McKillip's Tavern 131
McLaughlin, Dewit 194
McMahon, Barb 204
Meacham, Dr. 177
Menomonie, Wis. 206
*Merck's 1899 Manual of the Materia
    Medica* (book) 143
Meridean 27
Merrill, Wis. 154, 156
Mickey's Tavern 92
Miller, Mr. 168
Millevolte, Vinny 203
Millevolte Recording Studio 203
Mills, Charlotte 198
Mill Creek 207
Milwaukee, Wis. 33, 55, 68, 157,
    163, 169, 175, 179, 181,
    182, 189, 190, 193
Milwaukee Children's Hospital 163
Milwaukee Journal (newspaper) 182
Milwaukee Journal Sentinel (news-
    paper) 180
Mineral Point, Wis. 207
Mississagi Strait 139
Mississippi River 137
Moore, Verna 200
Mount Ida, Wis. 208

N

Nashotah, Wis. 167, 208
Nashotah House 165
Nehring, Bill 215
Nekoosa, Wis. 208
Nelsen's Hall 214
New Age Radio 50
New Moon Café 209
New Zealand, country of 141
Niagara 137
Norman, Michael 148, 162, 180

Northern Pacific Railroad 155
Notz, Dr. E.J.W. 190
Nyack, the 183

O

O'Brien, Mike 79
Oconomowoc, Wis. 168, 209
Octagon House 202
Old Baraboo Inn 196
Olshanski, Kristen 87
Ontario Street (Madison, Wis.) 97
Oshkosh, Wis. 209, 210
Outagamie County, Wis. 194
Ozaukee County, Wis. 202

P

Paige, Mrs. 209
Papazoglakis, Tom 167
Parker, Kristin 101
Pearl, Joseph 181
Pecatonica River 210
Peoria, Ill 137
Petoskey (ship) 182
Pewaukee, Wis. 167
Phillips, Wis. 201, 210
Pilot Island 140
Plainfield, Wis. 210
Plainfield Cemetery 211
Pleasant Ridge, Wis. 211
Polk County, Wis. 194
Pooley, Will 153
Pope, Daniel 166
Portage, Wis. 211
Portage County 194, 212, 213
Potosi, Wis. 211
Potosi Brewery 211
Prairie du Chien, Wis. 211
Price County, Wis. 201, 210
Priest, A.W. 194
Prohibition 92, 168, 191
Proof Positive (book) 34
Protection (tugboat) 183

R

Ramada Plaza Hotel 191
Ranieri, Paul 157, 159

Ransome, Ralph and Dorothy 146, 147
Ravensholme 142
Reedsburg, Wis. 212
Reidy House 110
Reilly House 132
Rhode Opera House 205
Rider, Geri 127
Ridgeway, Wis. 129, 131
Robinson, Dr. Chauncey C. 179
Rock County, Wis. 201
Roger the Terrible 78
Roll, Todd 19, 23
Rothschild, Wis. 22
Russell, George 133

S

S.S. Milwaukee (ship) 237
S.S. Titanic (ship) 156
Sacagawea 210
Sampson's Saloon and Hotel 130
Sand Hill Cemetery 25
Sardon, A.R. 237
Sauk County, Wis. 115, 196, 212
Sauk Prairie, Wis. 78
Sawyer County, Wis. 204
Schlais, Mark K. 201
Schneider, Kathleen 73
Schroeder, Walter 193
Schumacher, David 32
Scott, Beth 148, 162, 180
Scott, T. B. 155
Seymour, Wis. 127
Shawano County, Wis. 127
Sheboygan County, Wis. 202
Sheeley House 197
Shipwrecked Brew Pub 200
Showboat Saloon 214
Silver Moon 73
Sisters of Mercy of the Holy Cross 156
Smith, Scott Hunter 73
Soldiers Grove, Wis. 212
Sorden, L.G. 129
Southern Wisconsin Paranormal Research Group 32, 88
Southwick, Samuel 207
South Haven, Mich. 183

South Milwaukee, Wis. 144
Spaulding House Antique shop 36
Spiegel, Mary 176
Spiritland Cemetery 194
Spiritual Reality Investigators (SRI) 50, 56
Spirit of Geneva Lakes 165
Spring Brook Lutheran Church 26
St. Bartholomew Episcopal Church 167
St. Joseph, Mich. 181
Stateline Paranormal Investigative Network 57
Stevens Point, Wis. 212, 213
Stines, Captain Edward 181
Stonehouse, Frederick 186
Straits of Mackinac 186
Straz Hall 163
Subway Restaurant 199
Summerwind Mansion 148
Sun Prairie, Wis. 105

T

T.B. Scott Mansion 154
Tainter, Mabel 206
Taylor, Troy 154, 180, 236
Texas, state of 168
The Carver Effect (book) 151
The Legend of Sleepy Hollow (book) 130
The Shinning (book) 150
The Stolen Years (book) 87
The Wisconsin Road Guide to Haunted Locations (book) 24
Thurston, Herbert 180
Tomahawk, Wis. 99, 100
Tomlin, Amy 57
Touhey, Roger 86, 87
Tubey, Mary 189
Tylenol 68

U

U. S. Army 168
Uniroyal 199
Unsolved Mysteries (TV show) 25, 202

V

Varsity Theater 163
Vernon County, Wis. 120, 202
Vilas County, Wis. 148, 206
Villisca, Iowa 34

W

Walker, Calvert 208
Walker House 207
Walnut Grove Cemetery 202
Walton, Tom 187, 188
Walworth County, Wis. 43
Washington County, Wis. 203, 204
Washington D.C. 149
Washington Island 117, 118, 137,
        140, 214
Waukesha County, Wis. 142, 203,
        208, 209
Wausau, Wis. 15, 22, 110, 153
Wausau Paranormal Research Soci-
        ety 15, 23
Waushara County, Wis. 210
Wautoma, Wis. 211
Weird Wisconsin (book) 40
West Bay Lake, Wis. 148, 153
Wheaton, Ill. 191
Whiskers Olde Tyme Inn 202
Whispering Oaks Restaurant 164
White Noise (movie) 59
Whitewater, Wis. 42
Wille, Arthur 175
Winnebago County, Wis. 209, 210
Wisconsin Dells, Wis. 214, 215
Wisconsin Leather Company 177
Wisconsin Lore (book) 129
Wisconsin Rapids, Wis. 215
Wisconsin Road Guide to Haunted
        Locations 199
WMYX (radio) 50
WOLF (radio) 199
Wolf, Ray 204
Wonder Bar 32, 87
Woodman, Wis. 216
Woodville Cemetery 212
Wood County, Wis. 215
Worden, Bernice 210
World War I 143, 168

World War II 208

Y

YMCA 203

Z

Ziegler, Patty 202
Zuelke, Irving 195
Zuelke Building 195